EH ESSENTIAL HISTORIES

THE COLLAPSE OF YUGOSLAVIA 1991–99

Alastair Finlan

OSPREY PUBLISHING

Bloomsbury Publishing Plc
Kemp House, Chawley Park, Cumnor Hill, Oxford OX2 9PH, UK
29 Earlsfort Terrace, Dublin 2, Ireland
1385 Broadway, 5th Floor, New York, NY 10018, USA
E-mail: info@ospreypublishing.com
www.ospreypublishing.com

OSPREY is a trademark of Osprey Publishing Ltd

First published in Great Britain in 2022

The text in this edition is revised and updated from: ESS 63: *The Collapse of Yugoslavia 1991–1999* (Osprey Publishing, 2004).

A catalogue record for this book is available from the British Library.

ISBN: PB 9781472851246;
eBook 9781472851239;
ePDF 9781472851222;
XML 9781472851253

22 23 24 25 26   10 9 8 7 6 5 4 3 2 1

Maps by The Map Studio, revised by J B Illustrations
Index by Janet Andrew
Typeset by PDQ Digital Media Solutions, Bungay, UK
Printed and bound in India by Replika Press Private Ltd.

Osprey Publishing supports the Woodland Trust, the UK's leading woodland conservation charity.

To find out more about our authors and books visit www.ospreypublishing.com. Here you will find extracts, author interviews, details of forthcoming events and the option to sign up for our newsletter.

CONTENTS

INTRODUCTION

By the time this new edition is published in 2022, nearly twenty years will have passed between the original version written in 2003 and today. Much needs to be updated, but disturbingly, much has not changed at all. Sadly, the extraordinary events of the last two decades such as the Global War on Terror, the bloody fighting in Afghanistan and Iraq, the brutal rise and fall of the so-called Islamic State, Brexit, Trump and the ongoing Covid-19 global pandemic have collectively contributed to shifting the gaze of the international community away from the former Yugoslavia. At the surface level, the situation looks much better than it was with a significant amount of investment in the region in terms of rebuilding critical infrastructure such as the famous Mostar Bridge in 2004, but deep political and social fissures remain in the communities. Unsurprisingly, the scars of the visceral and intimate fighting between neighbours, who spoke the same language, shared a collective Yugoslav culture and often grew up together, are still visible in the consciousness of people that endured Europe's worst political failure since World War II.

The collapse of Yugoslavia from 1991 to 1999 represents one of the greatest yet least understood tragedies of recent times. After the fall of the Berlin Wall and the end of the Cold War, the rest of Eastern Europe embraced with enthusiasm the opportunity to move forward beyond the ravages of communism. The Balkans, however, seemed to step backwards. The region seemed unable to shake off the history of conflict and violence which had oppressed it for so long – it is often forgotten that Yugoslavia endured not only a German occupation but also a bitter civil war during World War II, in

OPPOSITE A JNA unit comprised of self-propelled artillery, trucks and armoured vehicles deployed near the border between Slovenia and Croatia in early 1991. (Photo by Peter Turnley/Corbis/VCG via Getty Images)

Bosniak fighters pose for a group photo near Guca Gora in 1993. The mixture of uniforms, weapons and youth reveals much about the problems facing non-Serb forces in BiH in equipping their military units. (Photo by Patrick ROBERT – Corbis/ Sygma via Getty Images)

which about one million people died. Perhaps, then, it was unsurprising (yet still shocking) that painful reminders of the brutality of World War II, like concentration camps, should re-emerge in Yugoslavia some 50 years later. Estimates today based on contemporary research suggest that around 140,000 people (it was estimated to be a quarter of a million in 2003) died in the savage ethnic fighting during the 1990s, and the international community watched in disbelief as genocide found new life in a modern age. Unlike other recent wars, the fighting in Yugoslavia was not dominated by high technology and detachment from the enemy. Instead, people killed those they knew, neighbour versus neighbour, and often with short-range weapons such as rifles, knives, or in some cases, pitchforks. It was a return to a type of warfare that seemed medieval in comparison to the state-of-the-art, satellite-guided bombs and cruise missiles that are the hallmarks of modern military operations.

The international effects of the bloody disintegration of Yugoslavia have been substantial and wide-ranging, and they are still evident in contemporary global affairs. Millions of refugees fled from the region into other parts of Europe, with profound social and economic consequences for their host countries. The influx of refugees was not only an unwelcome financial burden, but also sparked unrest in countries that were forced to absorb people with a completely different set of norms and values.

Multi-national operations involving thousands of stabilisation troops and billions of dollars in expenditure have been conducted in Bosnia and Herzegovina, Kosovo and Macedonia. These large-scale operations have been greatly reduced in size and in many cases handed over to much smaller EU forces such as *EUFOR Operation ALTHEA* in Bosnia and Herzegovina. The crimes committed during the fighting have also been brought to justice through the International Criminal Tribunal for the former Yugoslavia (ICTY), set up in 1993 at The Hague to address the serious violation of international humanitarian law.

The events in Yugoslavia in the 1990s possess an enigmatic quality. At the heart of the debate is the question of how people who have lived for years in peace can suddenly start killing each other in the most barbaric ways. Surely humanity at the latter end of the twentieth century had evolved beyond such practices, condemned by the international community after World War II?

The suffering in the Balkans thrust several key international figures into the limelight, whose reputations were largely sullied by either direct involvement in the killings, or their inability to generate a comprehensive solution to the crisis. Overnight, a little-known Serbian leader, Slobodan Milosevic, became a household name across the world. Many historians believe that Milosevic was a central figure in the outbreak of fighting between the different ethnic communities, yet

Indictment
2 counts of GENOCIDE (1 and 2)
5 counts of CRIMES AGAINST HUMANIT
4 counts of VIOLATIONS OF THE LAWS
OR CUSTOMS OF LAWS
The Trial
497 Trial days
337 Prosecution witnesses
248 Defence witnesses
1 Chamber witness

A remarkable historical event that few imagined possible during the fighting. Protestors stand witness to the trial of Ratko Mladic for war crimes, genocide and crimes against humanity. (Photo by Michel Porro/Stringer/Getty Images)

throughout the 1990s the international community was more than willing to negotiate with Milosevic as a legitimate authority rather than as a perpetrator of violence. Milosevic died of a heart attack while on trial for crimes against humanity in an EU prison in 2006.

Milosevic's Bosnian Serb partners, the flamboyant Radovan Karadzic and his ruthless military compatriot General Ratko Mladic, were also eventually brought to justice by the international community and are now convicted war criminals serving long jail sentences in EU prisons. Other regional leaders, such as Franjo Tudjman of Croatia and Alija Izetbegovic of Bosnia-Herzegovina, became equally well known in the global media, but with less notoriety than their Serbian counterparts. For the wider international community, unlike previous crises such as the Gulf War of 1991, no single international leader (until President Bill

Clinton in 1995) took the lead concerning policy towards the former Yugoslavia. However, some political analysts have raised serious questions about the role of the British leader John Major and his Foreign Secretary, Douglas Hurd, in ensuring that the European Community did not become too heavily involved at the outset of the fighting. By contrast, John Major's successor, Tony Blair, played a central part in ensuring swift military intervention in Kosovo in 1999, but his reputation too has been sullied for his part in involving Britain in the legally 'contested' invasion of Iraq in 2003.

The international community sent many high-level mediators to try to resolve the conflict in Yugoslavia, all with distinguished political pedigrees. The first was Lord Carrington, and others included eminent statesmen such as Cyrus Vance, Lord Owen, and Thorvald Stoltenberg. Towards the mid-1990s, the key negotiator was the United States Assistant Secretary of State, Richard Holbrooke, who was instrumental in bringing about the Dayton Agreement of 1995, and played a key role during negotiations over the Kosovo crisis in 1999. Many outstanding soldiers with illustrious careers, such as the Canadian General Lewis MacKenzie, General Philippe Morillon from France, and Britain's General Sir Michael Rose, were sent by their respective nations to take charge on the ground, yet all found the political context in the region very challenging. The twisted political web between the various Yugoslav factions, allied with the reluctance of outside countries to adopt a more robust peacekeeping posture, left soldiers on the ground brutally exposed, physically and mentally, to the horrors of ethnic conflict. Other military leaders fared better due to their willingness to grasp the Balkan nettle, such as the British generals Sir Rupert Smith and Sir Michael Jackson, and General Wesley Clark from the United States of America.

The role of the United Nations during the collapse of Yugoslavia has been heavily criticised, for allowing genocide to flourish under the guns of its soldiers sent to protect the victims. The most searing example of this neglect was the handing over of the town of Srebrenica to Bosnian Serb soldiers led by General Mladic, by a battalion of Dutch peacekeepers in 1995. Estimates suggest that, despite promising not to harm the remaining residents, Mladic's men killed around 8,000 Muslims (the estimate in 2003 was 7,000 but more victims have since been identified) in a carefully organised massacre. All three Secretary Generals who held office between 1991 and 1999, Javier Perez de Cuellar, Boutros Boutros-Ghali, and Kofi Annan (the head of the UN peacekeeping department during much of this period), have faced intense criticism for their actions or inactions during the bloodletting. Tens of thousands of UN soldiers from all around the world were deployed to the region under the title United Nations Protection Force (UNPROFOR), first to Croatia and then to Bosnia-Herzegovina. By the end of the mid-1990s, the influence of the United Nations began to be supplanted by that of the North Atlantic Treaty Organisation (NATO). Although this organisation appeared to lose its basic purpose with the end of the Cold War, and despite having been in existence since 1949, it fired its first shots in anger in 1994 in the former Yugoslavia. NATO would take a key position in bringing a cessation to the violence in the region, first in Bosnia in 1995, and then in Kosovo in 1999.

The haunting sadness of the Srebrenica-Potocari Memorial and Cemetery in 2018 dedicated to the memory of the victims of the Srebrenica massacre. (Photo by Adem Mehmedovic/ Anadolu Agency/ Getty Images)

BACKGROUND TO WAR

The collapse of Yugoslavia

The build-up to war in the former Yugoslavia in the 1990s is surrounded by myth and misunderstanding. One of these myths suggests that the enmity between the different nationalities had been festering for centuries, and periodically manifesting itself in random ethnic violence. In other words, they had always been killing each other and no amount of outside intervention would have weaned them off this abhorrent preoccupation. Unfortunately, badly informed sociological appraisals of this nature did nothing to halt the violence, but instead offered convenient excuses either to avoid or to limit involvement in the region. These misunderstandings were further reinforced by popular history. Yugoslavia has a unique significance in modern history as the 'Balkan Spark' that led to the outbreak of World War I. In 1914, a Bosnian Serb extremist called Gavrilo Princip managed in a remarkable fashion (given the ineptitude of his initial attempts) to kill Archduke Franz Ferdinand of Austria-Hungary in Sarajevo. Popular notions suggest that this event, in isolation, was the cause of World War I in which 10 million people died. This simplistic idea repeated and regurgitated by schools and universities across war-scarred nations like Britain, France and Germany belied the fact that

the event was hijacked by the great powers for their own ends. In other words, even if Princip had failed in his assassination attempt, war was likely to occur given the rigid timetable of the German Schlieffen Plan, the great military strategy to defeat France in a matter of weeks before turning to face the Russians. Nevertheless, myth replaced reality, and the region developed an unwarranted reputation as a place in which violence could spread uncontrollably outwards.

Yugoslavia has always been a complex mix of nations and autonomous areas: in the 1990s it comprised Bosnia-Herzegovina, Croatia, Kosovo, Macedonia, Montenegro, Serbia, Slovenia, and Vojvodina. It also plays host to diverse religions – Catholicism, Islam and Orthodox Christianity. In historical terms, however, it is a relatively new entity, born out of the aftermath of World War I. Prior to the Great War, the region was divided between two vast empires: the Ottoman Empire that had conquered much of the region in the fourteenth century (hence the Islamic influence in areas such as Bosnia-Herzegovina), and the Austrian-Hungarian Empire that would gain more territory from the rapidly weakening Ottomans as the years passed. Ironically, World War I sounded the death knell for both hegemonic empires, and the Treaty of Versailles in 1919 confirmed the new Kingdom of Serbs, Croats and Slovenes (renamed Yugoslavia in 1929). However, the events of World War II probably have more significance for the collapse of Yugoslavia in the 1990s than much older historical causes for conflict in the region. It was inevitable that Hitler and Mussolini would turn their attention to the Balkans, and they finally resorted to the war option in 1941. The Yugoslav response to the attack was fractured along ethnic lines that led quickly to civil war.

In Croatia, whose borders now expanded to encompass much of Bosnia-Herzegovina, the Axis powers supported a minority fascist group called the Ustasha, led by Ante Pavelic, which started to kill non-Croats and those who refused to

OPPOSITE A charred Croatian flag hangs in the disputed area of Travnik in 1993. The town became a flashpoint of tension between the Bosniaks and Bosnian Croats in BiH during the civil war. (Photo by Patrick ROBERT – Corbis/Sygma via Getty Images)

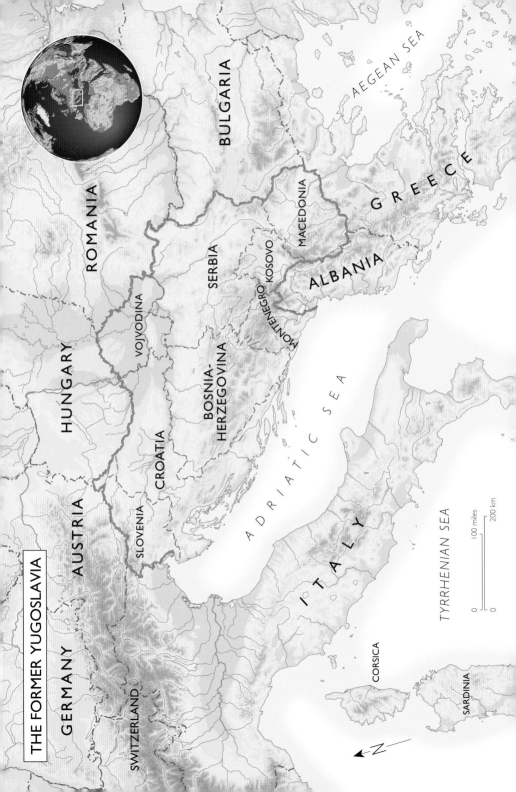

THE FORMER YUGOSLAVIA

AEGEAN SEA

BULGARIA

ROMANIA

GREECE

MACEDONIA

SERBIA

KOSOVO

ALBANIA

MONTENEGRO

VOJVODINA

HUNGARY

BOSNIA-
HERZEGOVINA

CROATIA

A D R I A T I C   S E A

SLOVENIA

AUSTRIA

ITALY

GERMANY

SWITZERLAND

TYRRHENIAN SEA

CORSICA

SARDINIA

100 miles

200 km

N

convert to Catholicism. Around half a million Serbs were killed in this period, many in notorious concentration camps such as Jasenovac. In the rest of Yugoslavia, the two major resistance movements against the Nazi occupiers were the Royalists, or Chetniks, who were led by Serb Colonel Draza Mihailovic representing a government that had fled in exile to London, and the Communists led by Josip Broz Tito. By the end of the bloody civil war, Tito emerged triumphant and led a united Yugoslavia (through sheer force of will) into the post-war period.

OPPOSITE The former Yugoslavia comprised the republics of Bosnia-Herzegovina, Croatia, Macedonia, Montenegro, Serbia, and Slovenia, and the autonomous regions of Kosovo and Vojvodina.

Josip Broz Tito

Tito's Yugoslavia developed a unique position in the Cold War. It was clearly a communist state, and yet it held good relations with the United States and Western Europe after Tito fell out with Stalin in 1948 (over Tito's opposition of Soviet policies). It also became a central player in the development of the Non-Aligned Movement during the Cold War, which offered predominantly developing countries an alternative option to siding with one superpower or the other, to avoid being caught up in the intense rivalry. On the surface, Yugoslavia was a thriving region after 1945, with good economic growth and firm political direction from Tito. In reality, the tensions that were exacerbated during World War II still existed, but circumstances forced them underground. Externally, the mixed relationship with the Soviet Union meant that, should Yugoslavia descend into chaos, the Red Army would in all likelihood roll across the border as it had done in Czechoslovakia in 1968 to restore 'order'. Such an event would result in the loss of all forms of political autonomy for the major political movements in whatever Yugoslav nation. It was simply a 'no-win' situation that everyone recognised, and Yugoslav defence policy was developed primarily to impede a Soviet occupation. Internally,

An elderly President Tito with one of his trademark (usually Cuban) cigars in 1979. (Bettmann/Getty Images)

Tito ruthlessly purged any flowerings of nationalism that threatened the Yugoslav federation. An upsurge of Croatian nationalism in the early 1970s was stamped on by Tito using typically repressive measures, such as troops and secret police. In addition, further nationalistic steam was released from the region by the setting up of the 1974 constitution, which created a revolving presidency, permitting all nations to lead the federation in rotation.

The death of Tito in 1980 did not provoke an immediate disintegration of Yugoslavia. His constitution appeared to continue to work well, and the threat from the Soviet Union, which had just invaded Afghanistan in 1979, was also quite apparent. However, signs of splits became increasingly evident as the Yugoslav economy began to worsen and nationalistic tendencies began to emerge on a more flagrant basis. The most notable of these was an inflammatory paper by the Serbian Academy of Sciences in 1986, claiming that President Tito, whose parents were from Croatia and Slovenia respectively, was prejudiced against Serbs and his new constitution held an anti-Serb bias by giving the regions of Kosovo and Vojvodina (traditionally Serb-controlled areas) autonomous status. The basic thrust of the memorandum (as it was called) suggested that Serbia's economic problems were a direct consequence of these two factors. The preferred solution was the creation of a Greater Serbia. In Kosovo, nationalistic tendencies amongst the Kosovo Albanian majority (90 per cent of the population in the 1980s) were becoming increasingly apparent as a response to the Serb domination of politics, and the presence of Serb police and soldiers in the province. To Serbia, Kosovo held a symbolic and cultural significance of mythical proportions. At the battle of Kosovo Polje in 1389, the Serb Army was defeated by the invading Ottomans. This battle is often cited (usually by Serbian extremists) as the supreme example of how Serbia was fighting to preserve Christianity in Europe against the invading tide of Islam. That said, despite the symbolism of the battle and, of course, the onset of the modern age, by the 1980s many Serbs were leaving Kosovo in fear of the ethnically fuelled violence and intimidation.

Slobodan Milosevic

It is impossible to ignore the role of Slobodan Milosevic in the disintegration of Yugoslavia in this critical period, and the Kosovo issue was his platform to power in the region. Born in Serbia of Montenegran parents (who, it is alleged, committed suicide), Milosevic studied law before moving into banking. His wife and childhood sweetheart, Dr Mirjana Markovic, a radical militant Marxist sociology lecturer, is often portrayed as his closest adviser. In the late 1980s, Milosevic, then leader

RIGHT The main driving force behind the violence in the former Yugoslavia, Slobodan Milosevic, as the fighting deepened across the region in 1993. (Antonio RIBEIRO/ Gamma-Rapho/ Getty Images)

of the Serbian League of Communists, travelled to Kosovo and in front of cheering Serbs and national media declared his support for them. From this moment onwards, Milosevic broke Europe's most important but unwritten political taboo (after the horrors of World War II) – he played the nationalist card. Overnight, Milosevic, or 'Slobo' as crowds used to refer to him, became a magnet for Serbian aspirations and ambitions. His speeches were popular with the masses, and highly persuasive. Propaganda was an essential part of his strategy, drawing upon Serbian history and the battle of Kosovo Polje to promote his cause. By the end of the 1980s, Milosevic had managed to annul Kosovo's autonomous status and forcibly suppress Kosovo Albanian protests against his actions. In Vojvodina – the autonomous region to the north of Serbia – the Serb strong man had already ensured that his own people were already firmly in control of the region.

Milosevic's actions in both Kosovo and Vojvodina caused immense concern amongst the other republics of the Yugoslav federation, most notably Croatia and Slovenia. It is important at this juncture to put the breakdown of the former Yugoslavia into a wider context in Eastern Europe. The end of the Cold War allowed the former communist-dominated states to stretch out their hands to the European Community (EC) as a means of providing long-term economic stability for their impoverished countries. States such as Slovenia and Croatia quite naturally saw this route as the logical solution to their economic woes, but the question was how to facilitate a new partnership given their status within the Yugoslav federation. It was this issue that dominated the critical meeting of Yugoslav Communists in January 1990. The leaders of Slovenia and Croatia put forward their plan for greater political pluralism and sovereignty for the republics. Milosevic, however, rejected the proposal, as it would diminish Belgrade's grip on the federation. The upshot of the meeting was deadlock. The leaders of Croatia and Slovenia walked out and promised to hold multi-party elections as soon as possible.

Imbalance of power

Elections were held in 1990 across the various republics of Yugoslavia. In Croatia, the nationalist Franjo Tudjman was brought to power. His policies generated immense fear in the half a million Serbs who lived in Croatia (12 per cent of the population) and who had long memories of the killings of non-Croats by Ustasha fascists in the 1940s. In Serbia, Milosevic stole almost $2 billion from the Federal Bank of Yugoslavia to fund his election campaign, and was brought to power as President. In Slovenia, the reformer and pro-EC Milan Kucan was elected President. In Bosnia-Herzegovina, the republic with the most mixed nationalities (44 per cent Muslim, 31 per cent Serb, 17 per cent Croat, and 5 per cent

NEXT PAGES A well-armed Croatian militiaman engages the JNA outside of Karlovac. The impressive firepower on display around the militiaman reveals the better situation in Croatia in gaining access to weaponry during the fighting. (Photo by Antoine GYORI – Corbis/Sygma via Getty Images)

Yugoslav), Alija Izetbegovic became President. In Macedonia, Kiro Gligorov was elected, and Momir Bulatovic attained power in Montenegro. Sidelined by these electoral results was the old Yugoslav federal structure that still remained active but increasingly became marginalised or compromised. The Prime Minister of the Yugoslav Federation, Ante Markovic, tried hard to resolve the economic problems but experienced increasing difficulty as the power of the centre diminished. The revolving Presidency essentially collapsed in May 1991, when the Serb President, Borisav Jovic, refused to stand aside for the incoming Croatian President, Stipe Mesic. Other institutions, like the Yugoslav People's Army (JNA) were, on paper, organisations designed to protect the federal structure and maintain the balance of power between the different republics. Increasingly, however, a hardcore of senior officers openly sided with the Serb position, to the point that any stance of neutrality was purely illusory.

The final nail in the coffin of the Yugoslav federation was the issue of independence. On 25 June 1991, Croatia and Slovenia declared their independence. War broke out between the JNA and Slovenia two days later. Despite the Brioni Agreement negotiated by the EC and Yugoslavia on 7 July 1991, which ended the fighting in Slovenia, violence spread throughout Croatia in the following months. In spring 1992, after the declaration of independence by Bosnia-Herzegovina, war broke out in that republic as well. The dream of Yugoslav integrity died over the issue of independence from 1991 to 1992.

International intervention

This brewing crisis in Yugoslavia occurred at a time of great debate in the international community about the issue of intervention in the new post-Cold War era. During the Cold War, a new style of operations had emerged that became known as 'peacekeeping'. It was, and still remains, a confusing concept. Ostensibly it means to keep the peace, but that is a misconception. In fact, peacekeeping evolved in the 1950s and 1960s as a response by the international community to ensure that proxy wars and rivalry between the two superpowers, usually in developing countries, did not escalate to the point of a third world war. Put simply, peacekeeping was not about stopping the violence (although it was a desirable outcome), but more about trying to minimise the fighting so that protagonists would eventually be happy to set aside their weapons and seek a political solution. Consequently, the role of UN forces in peacekeeping was a delicate one that required a non-threatening posture (light weapons and vehicles), a ruthless adherence to impartiality and, most importantly, the consent of all warring sides to conduct humanitarian operations in the war zone. Peacekeeping forces structured along these lines are not designed for offensive operations (though they can carry them out if necessary) and consequently, if attacked by one side or another, have distinct vulnerabilities. These sorts of operations fall under the modern military term of peace support operations (PSO) – a sliding scale of options from peacekeeping to peace enforcement, which, as the term suggests, is the robust use of force to achieve peace. In peace enforcement, impartiality and consent are thrown out, and UN forces impose their will on the conflict. Dividing the two ends of the sliding scale is the notional 'Mogadishu Line', named after the infamous incident in Somalia in 1993, when 18 US soldiers were killed. During the 1990s, enormous debate was taking place within the military forces of the United States and their NATO partners as to the nature of the Mogadishu Line. Was it fixed (and once crossed then the peacekeeping operation would have to be abandoned), or was it flexible depending on the situation? If the latter, then UN forces could apply a little force to

NATO secures the peace. An American soldier from NATO's powerful Implementation Force (IFOR) is deployed to enforce the peace in Bosnia from 31 December 1995 onwards. (Photo by ODD ANDERSEN/AFP via Getty Images)

achieve their objectives and then fall back to a peacekeeping role. This debate was at the forefront of military thinking in Europe and the United States while UN forces were wrestling with the destabilising situation in Yugoslavia from 1991 to 1995.

WARRING SIDES

The uneven contest

Multiple protagonists

One of the most fascinating and yet confusing aspects of the breakdown of the former Yugoslavia was the sheer number of participants involved in the fighting. Usually, wars involve just two major protagonists, but in the Balkans at least thirteen players in the conflict (active and passive to varying degrees) can be clearly identified. These participants included Bosnian Croats, Bosnian Muslims (known as the Bosniacs or Bosniaks after 1993) and Bosnian Serbs, Croatians, Croatian Serbs, Kosovans, Macedonians, Montenegrins, Serbians, Slovenians, Vojvodinans, not to mention the North Atlantic Treaty Organisation (NATO) and the United Nations. These collective identities and bodies represented the official parties, but on the ground other organisations, such as non-governmental agencies, and unofficial groups comprising bandits, mercenaries and criminal gangs, added to the complexity of the situation. Overall, it was an extremely tangled web of interests that, for many observers, seemed simply impenetrable.

Prior to the disintegration of the federation into bloody conflict, the most powerful military formation had been the Yugoslav People's Army, commonly referred to as the

JNA (Jugoslovenska Narodna Armija). This was a regular formation that possessed the usual components of an air force, navy and ground forces. Supporting the regulars was a territorial reserve formation called the Territorial Defence Force, or TO (Teritorijalna Odbrana). This was a military formation that specialised in guerrilla warfare in the same manner as the wartime partisans. The JNA was stationed throughout Yugoslavia and drew its recruits from all the regions. By the 1990s, it was almost completely self-sufficient in terms of weapons production across the whole spectrum of military hardware, from rifles to battlefield rockets. Indeed, the Yugoslav weapons industry (producing copies of reliable Soviet types) provided a lucrative source of foreign currency due to their popularity with the international arms trade – a relationship that continues to the present day.

Serbian forces

Serbia was the most powerful nation in the region, and the source of Serbia's military strength stemmed from the covert bias of the JNA officer corps towards Milosevic. Interestingly, in 1991 the Minister of Defence, General Kadijevic, and his Chief of Staff, General Adzic, were Serbs from Croatia and Bosnia. In this respect, the JNA had broken with its long-standing tradition of political neutrality and loyalty to the federation rather than to a single nation. This process was evident through various reforms to the structure and disposition of the JNA throughout Yugoslavia at the end of the 1980s, giving the military more autonomy from regional political bodies. In turn, this facilitated the JNA in helping the diverse pockets of Serbs in different parts of Yugoslavia, such as Croatia and Bosnia-Herzegovina, when the fighting broke out. In 1992, the JNA was reorganised into the Army of Yugoslavia, or VJ, and the Army of the Serbian Republic (Bosnia-Herzegovina), otherwise known as the VRS. In addition, another formation –

the Armed Forces of the Republic of Serbian Krajina (Croatia), or OS RSK – became active in the same year. Some historians have suggested that these institutional changes to the old JNA were a mask to conceal the direct assistance that it was giving to Serbs in Bosnia-Herzegovina and Croatia. In other words, Milosevic could pretend to international negotiators and politicians that his hands were clean of the bloodshed when in fact he was manipulating events on the ground through these new structures.

JNA T-55 tanks traversing open ground at the start of the hostilities. The remarkable T-54/55 family of tanks were produced in very large numbers and can still be found fighting in conflict zones today. (Photo by Peter Turnley/ Corbis/VCG via Getty Images)

On the surface, the regular Serb forces in whatever location and guise bore all the trappings of conventional military forces. Officers wore pressed uniforms and ostensibly were little different from their counterparts in international military formation such as NATO. This façade was perhaps one of the reasons why the international community and their military representatives deployed in the region found it psychologically easier to deal with the Serbs. Put simply, they looked little different from themselves.

Yugoslav forces

From a purely military perspective, the armed forces of Yugoslavia were reasonably well-equipped in every respect. Overall, the JNA had 180,000 active soldiers in 1990, and could double that number by calling up trained reservists in an emergency. It possessed slightly fewer than 2,000 tanks by the outbreak of the fighting, of which around 300 were the Yugoslav version of the formidable Soviet T-72, called the M-84, though the vast majority (almost half) were T-54s and T-55s. In addition, reserve stocks included significant quantities of World War II tanks, including 400 T-34s and 300 M-4 Shermans. Like all modern ground forces, the JNA had built up hundreds of armoured personnel carriers (APCs), from Soviet BTR-40s and 50s to BRDM-2s. Yugoslav artillery units boasted nearly 2,000 heavy weapons (both field guns and howitzers) made domestically, in the Soviet Union, or in the United States. These powerful units were also supported by 128mm rocket systems and a small number of Frog-7 battlefield missiles. Of equal significance for the future conflict, Yugoslav forces had over 6,000 mortars (82mm and 120mm), which were ideal weapons for light forces harassing or simply terrorising towns and villages. Anti-tank capabilities included recoilless rifles (57mm and 105mm) and Soviet AT-3 Sagger and AT-4 Spigot wire-guided anti-tank missiles. To offer protection from air threats, Yugoslav ground units were equipped with over 3,000 anti-aircraft guns that in many cases could be utilised in a ground attack role with their explosive-tipped shells wreaking enormous damage on houses and soft targets.

In the air, the Yugoslav Air Force had taken possession of the latest Soviet MiG-29 Fulcrum aircraft, and was considered a serious threat by NATO forces. However, only a small quantity of these aeroplanes (less than 20) had been purchased at the end of the 1980s. The vast majority of Yugoslav aircraft, just over a hundred in total, were old Soviet MiG-21 Fishbeds, which were supplemented by light attack aircraft such as the

The JNA gets ready for deployment, but its first operations in Slovenia were not very successful. (Photo by Antoine GYORI – Corbis/Sygma via Getty Images)

Orao 2 armed with US AGM-65 Maverick missiles, the Jastreb 2 (powered by Rolls Royce Viper engines) and the G-2 Galeb/G-4 Super Galeb. All of these aircraft could carry either 23mm GSh-23 cannon or 12.7mm machine guns as well as some light bombs and cluster munitions. The Yugoslav Air Force's rotary wing assets comprised around a hundred Mi-8 Hip transport helicopters, KA-25/KA-28 anti-submarine helicopters, and attack helicopters such as the Anglo-French Gazelle with anti-tank missiles. Yugoslavia's air defence network was formidable by the early 1990s, and offered both long-range and short-range anti-aircraft protection. Its missiles, both fixed and mobile, included SA-2 Guideline, SA-3 Goa, SA-6 Gainful, SA-7 Grail (Strela 2), and SA-11 Gadfly. These missiles were linked to a series of early warning and air defence radars scattered throughout the federation.

At sea, the Yugoslav Navy was geared along with the rest of armed forces to defend the federation, so its operations were largely of a coastal nature. Its most significant surface assets included a couple of Kotor and Koni class frigates with anti-ship and anti-air capabilities, and Osa and Koncar class missile boats. For underwater operations, the navy possessed five diesel-electric submarines, made up of the Heroj and Sava class boats with 533mm torpedo tubes. Alongside an eclectic collection of minesweepers and smaller patrol boats, the Yugoslav Navy possessed a sizeable quantity of large calibre coastal guns and land-based anti-ship missiles.

The covert alliance between the JNA and Serbia meant that the balance of the military advantage remained with Serbian forces throughout the entire conflict. This superiority was sustained, ironically, by the imposition of a UN arms embargo on the region on 25 September 1991. Arms embargoes are one means by which the international community can try to reduce the potential for fighting in a specific area. In the Balkans, the imposition merely allowed the Serbs to continue their brutal policies safe in the knowledge that their enemies did not have the military capabilities to stop them.

Croatian forces

In Croatia, the situation was very difficult for the anti-Serb forces in the early years of the fighting. The Croatian Army, the HV, was almost 100,000 strong with 200 tanks (mainly T-55s but some M-84s as well) and significant quantities of supporting artillery including 203mm guns. Sophisticated anti-tank missiles such as the Sagger and Spigot were also available, along with over 600 medium to heavy calibre (14.5mm to 30mm) machine guns. In addition, Croatian capabilities included anti-aircraft missiles, the largest quantity being 2,000 SA-7 man-portable missiles, some 300 aircraft (Mig-21s, Galebs and Jastrebs) and Mi-8 helicopters. At sea,

Croatia inherited some of the largest bases of the Yugoslav Navy, particularly at Split, with Koncar class and Osa class missile boats, a corvette and numerous smaller vessels.

Other players

Against these forces were arrayed the Armed Forces of the Republic of Serbian Krajina, or OS RSK, which was around 40-50,000 strong with 300 tanks (T-34/T-54/T-55) and APCs with 500 artillery guns of various calibres. To the north of Croatia, Slovenia – the catalyst for the fighting – had the smallest armed forces, just 15,000 soldiers with 150 tanks including significant numbers of M-84s and some supporting artillery and helicopters.

In Bosnia-Herzegovina the Serb forces, or VRS, had 50–80,000 soldiers, with around 300 tanks, the majority of which were the older T-55 types, and 400 APCs. Most significantly, the Bosnian Serbs had over 800 artillery guns, howitzers and mortars of various calibres. In contrast, the opposition in the form of the Bosniaks and Bosnian Croats were at a significant disadvantage. The more numerous Bosniak forces, or ABiH (Armed Forces of Bosnia-Herzegovina), numbering around 60,000 at the outbreak of the fighting and swelling to well over 100,000, had very little in terms of heavy firepower. By 1993, records suggest that Bosniak forces had just 20 tanks and 30 APCs, with only a few heavy artillery pieces. The Bosnian Croats, or HVO (Croatian Defence Council), possessed around 50,000 soldiers a year after war broke out, with just 50 tanks (mainly T-34 or T-55) and about 500 artillery guns of varying descriptions.

Overall, it was quite clear to all sides that Serbia and Serbian forces in Croatia and Bosnia-Herzegovina were much better equipped in terms of firepower in the form of aircraft, artillery and tanks than their regional foes. Nevertheless, the Serbs did not enough manpower or equipment to

NEXT PAGES
A motley band of Croatian militiamen in 1991 armed with a variety of weapons and uniforms take a break in Dubica. (Photo by Antoine GYORI – Corbis/ Sygma via Getty Images)

The horror of daily life in Sarajevo under the gaze of snipers. Bosniak fighters engage Serbian snipers while civilians seek cover in 1992. (MIKE PERSSON/ AFP via Getty Images)

produce a decisive military outcome across all of the regions of the former Yugoslavia. Instead, they had enough strength to hold on to their initial gains (when it was in their interest to do so) and repel or punish opposition forces that tried to break the status quo. This stark military imbalance provoked immense misery for those civilians of all nationalities caught up in the struggle between the warring sides. The absence of total victory meant that the cycle of violence, chaos and, to some observers, downright savagery continued at a slow pace for several years.

OUTBREAK

Stumbling into violence

The disintegration of the former Yugoslavia did not occur overnight. Nor did the nationalities of the federation instantaneously declare war on each other. Instead, a series of seemingly innocuous events began to generate a steady momentum of violence that would engulf Bosnia-Herzegovina just a year later. One such catalyst for disorder was the declaration of independence by Slovenia and Croatia on 25 June 1991, which prompted Yugoslav Prime Minister Ante Markovic (a Croat) to send the JNA to secure the international borders. Some historians suggest that the plan was an immense blunder, since Milosevic and Kucan had already agreed on Slovenia's departure from the Yugoslav federation – after all, the vast majority of the population were Slovenian. Croatia, however, with over 500,000 Serbs, was quite a different matter to Milosevic. Nevertheless, the JNA ran into serious difficulties in Slovenia when coming face-to-face with hostile resistance. Surprisingly, the initial deployment of the JNA was just two columns of motorised troops – about 2,000 soldiers in total – which perhaps reflected the degree to which the Yugoslav Prime Minister and the JNA leadership had underestimated the magnitude of the task. This level of disorganisation could also be construed as evidence of a lack of preplanning for such operations.

War in Slovenia and the Brioni Agreement

The Slovenian population was well prepared to deal with the threat of the JNA due to a huge anti-JNA propaganda campaign in the country, designed to have an impact not only domestically, but also internationally. Consequently, when the JNA was ordered to move, the Slovenian forces had plans to neutralise it. Slovenian strategy to deal with the JNA was simple and highly effective: columns of JNA soldiers would be surrounded and prevented from moving backwards or forwards by obstacles such as felled trees. The Slovenians, many of whom belonged to the TO organisation, would then open fire on the trapped columns, which were often made up of scared reservists who had no wish to be in Slovenia in the first place. In addition, the JNA barracks in Slovenia would be quickly surrounded and the remaining soldiers and their families subjected to intimidation. The fighting between the JNA and Slovenia lasted about a week, in which the majority of dead (just over 40) were JNA soldiers.

The war in Slovenia ended quickly, due to the swift intervention of the international community. Europe, in the form of the European Community (EC) and later as the European Union (EU), saw an opportunity with the crisis in Yugoslavia to assert itself in the new post-Cold War environment. It is easy to forget that events on the European continent since World War II had been determined and ultimately resolved by an outside power – the United States. The end of the Cold War, however, presented Europe with an opportunity to finally resolve its security problems by itself, and Yugoslavia seemed like an excellent place to start. The Brioni Agreement of 7 July 1991, brokered by the EC, ended the fighting between the JNA and Slovenia. In reality, this success merely papered over the widening cracks in the federal structure, and also gave credence to the notion that diplomacy could end fighting in the former Yugoslavia without recourse to the force option. Sadly, despite the early success with the

OPPOSITE The ill-fated JNA on operations in Slovenia. (Photo by Jacques Langevin/ Sygma via Getty Images)

fighting in Slovenia, neither Europe nor the United Nations demonstrated the will or capability to resolve the growing conflict in the former Yugoslavia. Tragically, the failure to deal decisively with the Balkan problem at the earliest possible stage condemned thousands of people to brutal deaths not in an instant, but rather at a slow-motion pace.

War spreads to Croatia

The Brioni Agreement ended the fighting in Slovenia, but by this stage violence was beginning to spread in Croatia. Initially, the tensions would manifest themselves through slogans, visual representations of identity such as flags hanging from specific houses or streets, threats and then the use of ethnic beatings, intimidation, broken windows and finally random killings, isolated at first before becoming apparent on a wider scale. Of course, none of this occurred in a vacuum – people need to be reminded of reasons to hate and, ultimately, to kill. In Croatia, for the minority Serb population (12 per cent in total) these reasons were provided by local politicians such as Lazar Macura, who was instrumental in the referendum as to whether the Serb pocket in Croatia should join with Serbia itself in political union. Macura's message to the Serbs of the Krajina was broadcast on a regular basis through Radio Knin, which became notorious for its inflammatory and racist programmes, designed to sow the seeds of mistrust between Croats and Serbs who had been living in peace side by side for decades. In fact, these early incidents mirrored how Milosevic himself dominated the Serbian media industry to the extent that people (apart from soldiers serving in Bosnia-Herzegovina and Croatia) had a completely divorced perspective on the havoc that Serbs were inflicting on their neighbours. The violence in Croatia spread not only geographically, but also in magnitude as the hatred between the two sides intensified with each new incident of violence. In addition, Croatian authorities engaged

An exhausted Croatian militiaman weary from battle outside of Karlovac. Combat provokes powerful emotions/physical effects on combatants through intense cycles of anxiety/fear/elation that create profound weariness. (Photo by Antoine GYORI – Corbis/Sygma via Getty Images)

in the highly questionable use of counter-propaganda and quite quickly a cycle of violence was set in motion.

Some Serbian writers suggest that the war in Croatia was started by Croats copying the successful Slovenian tactics in dealing with JNA forces. It is true that Croats used blockade tactics against the JNA, but the situation was very different. Firstly, the size of the JNA forces in Croatia was much larger, and secondly, unlike Slovenia, many Serb soldiers had a stake in Croatia. Interestingly, in contrast to this position, a significant number of the JNA soldiers stationed in Croatia were in fact Croats. However, Croatian propaganda persuaded many of these officers and soldiers to leave the JNA, which in itself prompted a higher degree of paranoia amongst the officer corps as to whom could they trust. The most surprising feature about the JNA strategy in Croatia was its incoherence in the initial stages as to the actual aims of the mission. Despite this lack of strategic direction, the military superiority of the JNA began to assert itself on the Croatian landscape, and vast areas of territory were secured in favour of the indigenous Serb population. Gradually, a pattern of tactics began to emerge on both sides that became universally known as ethnic cleansing: the deliberate destruction of property and life based on ethnic affiliation. Very quickly, the sight of burnt-out or burning villages became synonymous throughout the international news media with the former Yugoslavia.

International response

International reaction to the burgeoning crisis in the region was centred around the diplomacy of the EC, and various other concerned international organisations such as the Conference on Security and Cooperation in Europe (CSCE), the International Monetary Fund (IMF) and the Western European Union (WEU). The chief EC negotiator, Lord Carrington, and his UN counterpart, the American statesman Cyrus Vance, tried hard to mediate ceasefires but with little success on the ground. Serbia was quickly identified as a source of much of the fighting, which led to the imposition of sanctions in late 1991 with limited effect. The great debate in international political circles was whether to recognise the independence of Croatia and Slovenia. Britain, France and Lord Carrington argued against such a move, whereas the newly unified Germany, which had long-standing historical ties with Croatia, was in favour of recognising independence. It was an argument that Germany eventually won, and the EC recognised Croatia and Slovenia on 15 January 1992. This was a critical issue, because international recognition of the breakaway republics changed the character and nature

of the war raging in Croatia. Far from being an internal dispute or civil war, it now became an interstate conflict with international recognition. The United States was initially slow to follow the EC's lead with regard to the status of these two nations, and by spring 1992 Bosnia-Herzegovina had held its own referendum for independence. On 6 April, the EC recognised Bosnia-Herzegovina's independence, and the next day the United States formally recognised all three former members of the Yugoslav federation.

UNPROFOR establishes its footprint in the region. French UN forces arrive at the port of Rijeka in Croatia in 1992. (JOEL ROBINE/AFP/GettyImages)

It is frequently reported that war broke out in Bosnia-Herzegovina on the day that the EC recognised its independence, though some writers have argued that fighting was apparent in the last week of March. Milosevic took a particularly hard line with regard to Bosnia-Herzegovina, because he was simply not prepared to give up territory in a land in which Serbs comprised 31 per cent of the population, with the other major ethnic groups of Muslims and Croats making up 44 per cent and 17 per cent of the population respectively. By January 1992, a new player had emerged on the ground in the Balkans: the United Nations. In response to a brokered ceasefire, the UN had agreed to set up the United Nations Protection Force (UNPROFOR) in Croatia initially, though it would be extended to include Bosnia-Herzegovina as the fighting spread to that area. These forces, of which a sizeable component was from Britain (the Cheshire Regiment), were sent to the Balkans with a peacekeeping mandate only.

In other words, their tasks included trying to ensure that the ceasefire continued, escorting aid convoys into besieged areas, and acting as a trusted third-party mediator between the warring sides. A difficult and dangerous job at the best of times, but one to which a whole host of nations contributed, from countries as geographically diverse as Canada, France, Jordan, Russia and Nepal, to name but a few. Britain's initial contribution was limited to just under 2,000 soldiers under the title 'Operation *Grapple*'. However, their biggest assets, apart from troops on the ground, were their white-painted Warrior armoured personnel carriers armed with 30mm Rarden cannon that could hit targets with 'armour piercing discarding sabot' (APDS) shells at ranges of 2,000 yards. Overall, these responses were an attempt by the international community to manage the crisis on the ground in the former Yugoslavia, alongside ongoing international diplomacy to somehow bring about a firm resolution to the crisis.

Sadly, these attempts were merely delusions. The fighting and ethnic cleansing continued unabated, and in the summer of 1992 the old horror of concentration camps was revealed to the international community at Omarska. Once more, the spectre of European genocide rose up to face international politicians who, as their forebears had done in the 1930s, refused to fully commit to the force option to decisively resolve the problem on the ground. As such, they condemned millions of people in Bosnia-Herzegovina to a further three years of brutality, loss of dignity, and helplessness.

THE FIGHTING

The destruction of Yugoslavia

Chaos and crime

A source of great debate among historians studying the collapse of Yugoslavia is the degree to which the fighting was planned by the major leaders. One of the most notable and persuasive accounts of this turbulent time, entitled *The Serbian Project and its Adversaries: A Strategy of War Crimes* by Professor James Gow claims that Slobodan Milosevic had devised a 'project' to push the region into war, so that the much stronger Serb forces could ultimately carve out a Greater Serbia in parts of Croatia and Bosnia-Herzegovina. On the face of it, Serbia's spectacular gains in the early part of the fighting would support such a line of argument, but as the International Criminal Tribunal for the former Yugoslavia (ICTY) has found, it is very difficult to prove categorically that Milosevic's hand was behind the instability. Nevertheless, regardless of the causes of the conflict, the fighting in Yugoslavia stands apart from traditional warfare as a result of the deeply personal nature of the violence. Victims in many cases knew their attackers, either from sharing the same town or having spent time at school together. Neighbours who had lived for years in peace suddenly found themselves drawn, willingly in some respects and unwillingly in others, towards ethnic affiliations. Unlike previous conflicts in recent history, like the Gulf War of 1991, the boundary between civilians and soldiers became rapidly blurred as the battlefield stretched across cities, towns and villages.

As the chaos spread and law and order broke down, criminals flourished and, indeed, the criminalisation of the fighting in Yugoslavia is one of the main historical features of the conflict. Gangs of bandits and outlaws terrorised people to the same extent as soldiers in uniform. Anyone with a gun could set up roadblocks throughout the region, acting purely on their own initiative. These decentralised and criminalised facets of the wars in the former Yugoslavia made it immensely difficult for outside authorities such as the United Nations to negotiate a lasting ceasefire on the ground. Too many interests were at stake, official and unofficial, in the crime zone of Yugoslavia. Once the civil authorities and law-enforcing capabilities of the nations of Croatia and Bosnia-Herzegovina had been traumatically undermined by the activities of the JNA, then chaos and crime flourished as it would in any country throughout the world in which policemen and centralised authority had disappeared. This is the indelible

JNA forces cleaning up in Erdut. Erdut was the base of the notorious Serbian paramilitary Arkan in 1991 and witnessed mass expulsions and murder of civilians. (Photo by Antoine GYORI – Corbis/ Sygma via Getty Images)

stain of responsibility that Milosevic will bear as the politician who used the military instruments of the state to repress his fellow Yugoslavs in the most callously indifferent manner.

The war in Croatia
Serb groups and figureheads

There were many interested parties in the fighting in Croatia, but the instigators of the violence were certainly the Serbs. The spread of hatred and violence in the region revolved around figureheads whose backgrounds and appearance bordered on the absurd. A central figure in the rallying of Croatian Serbs to war was Milan Babic, a rotund former dentist who, through his powerbase in Knin, urged Croatian Serbs to resist what he labelled the fascist Ustasha regime of the newly elected Franjo Tudjman. On 25 August 1990, Babic declared the creation of the Autonomous Province of the Serbian Krajina, which inevitably placed the Serbs on a collision course with the democratically elected government of President Tudjman. However, the Serb pocket in Croatia had a very good reason to believe that it could prevail: it benefited enormously from the covert help of the JNA, which from 1990 onwards started to redistribute weapons from territorial units based in Croatia to the Serb population. Consequently, those Croatian police who were loyal to President Tudjman often found themselves completely outgunned when trying to restore order in Serb-dominated areas. In addition, Milosevic, though denying to the international community any involvement in the fighting in Croatia, offered direct help politically and militarily to the Croatian Serbs, including air power either to intimidate the Croatian police or to simply bomb parts of Croatia. President Tudjman himself, although draped with the trappings of Croatian nationalism (particularly the famous chequerboard flag), tried hard to avert outright war with the Serbs. Ultimately, however, events on the ground spiralled out of control.

Arkan's 'Tigers' in 1995 – a well-armed gang of paramilitaries with a reputation for brutality and ruthlessness. Arkan was a well-known international criminal before the fighting broke out in the former Yugoslavia. (AFP via Getty Images)

The fighting in Croatia intensified in late spring of 1991 in the region known as Eastern Slavonia on the border with Vojvodina, especially around the town of Vukovar. A key element in the intensification of violence carried out by Serbs in this part of Croatia was the use of extremist groups with strong links to Belgrade. The most notorious of these 'agitators of violence' were Arkan's 'Tigers' and Seselj's 'Chetniks'. Arkan, or Zeljko Raznjatovic, was an internationally renowned bank robber (his 'scores' included robberies in Belgium, Germany, Holland and Sweden) who was known to have links with the Yugoslav secret police. Other aspects of his curriculum vitae included managing the fan club of Belgrade's Red Star football club, known as the 'Delije', whose members became renowned for their thuggish and nationalistic behaviour. Arkan managed to combine the worst aspects of football hooliganism and tribalism with modern military weaponry. It was unsurprising that this fan club provided an excellent recruiting ground for the extraordinarily well-equipped Tigers, who rampaged with the utmost brutality through parts of Croatia and later Bosnia-Herzegovina under Arkan's leadership.

In contrast to the 'thug' background of Arkan, Vojislav Seselj was a radical Serb intellectual with a PhD to boot, who was more than happy to fuel ethnic tensions with irresponsible media statements designed to create fear and unrest. His followers (who included groups like the White Eagles) were modelled closely on the World War II Chetniks, a Serb nationalist resistance movement, and wore traditional hats with Eagle badges on the front. Both groups and their leaders were primarily criminals intent on pillage and murder in order to create as much chaos as possible. In this respect, they succeeded, and their activities on the eastern borders of Croatia were characterised by these units sweeping through villages and towns. In the case of the attack on the town of Baranja, they openly fought in concert with the JNA, and this combination of strength meant that Eastern Slavonia quickly fell under Serb control. So, too, did other neighbouring districts with the overt support of the JNA, and the town Vukovar acquired an internationally recognised name due to the significant media coverage of the strangling siege until its surrender on 17 November 1991.

The siege of cities

The fighting spread quite quickly to include the regions around the Serb Krajina and famous Croatian cities. In the South, Montenegran troops loyal to the JNA caused international outrage by shelling the coastal city of Dubrovnik, which had been a popular tourist destination for Western Europeans. The siege of Dubrovnik was heavily covered by the international media, drawing attention yet again to the role of the Serbs and their allies in this conflict. Zagreb, too, was subject to regular bombings by the Yugoslav Air Force. In the Krajina, a new figure emerged in the JNA forces as a ruthlessly efficient commander – Colonel (later promoted to General) Ratko Mladic was a Bosnian Serb whose father had been killed by the Ustasha during World War II.

Mladic was a brash, larger-than-life character who undoubtedly possessed an astute military mind (when facing weaker opposition), but his name quickly became associated with ethnic cleansing in the areas under his control. Initially, due to the massive imbalance of arms, the Croatian Serbs and the JNA held the military advantage and exploited it to the full. However, Croatia managed to access arms from countries such as Hungary (mainly light weapons and anti-aircraft guns) before the UN embargo (UNSC Resolution 713 on 25 September 1991). Even after the embargo was imposed, Croatia managed to illegally acquire some weapons due to the geography of the country – a long western seaboard, ideal for smugglers. Its borders with countries to the north also had potential for unofficial arms transactions. Consequently, although the Serb pockets in the Krajina and Eastern Slavonia were well established by the start of 1992, the Serbs simply did not have the military capability to take all of Croatia. Nevertheless, the fighting and widespread ethnic cleansing had set the tone for the forthcoming war in Bosnia-Herzegovina, and relations between Serbs and Croats would never be the same again.

A Croatian armoured personnel carrier leading a convoy of vehicles engaged in a battle with JNA forces in 1991. (DAVID BRAUCHLI/AFP via Getty Images)

The United Nations in the former Yugoslavia

The role of the United Nations in the Balkans has generated immense criticism, due to its inability to quickly stop the fighting. Forty-seven United Nations Security Council Resolutions were passed between April 1992 and October 1993, but none managed to halt the violence decisively. For instance, the famous, or infamous, arms embargo (UNSCR 713) failed to stop the fighting due to the indigenous arms production capacities of the former Yugoslavia, and the ability of some nationalities to smuggle weapons across the borders. A more involved approach by the international community occurred on 21 February 1992, when the first deployments of UN forces were sanctioned by the Security Council with 14,000 troops despatched to Croatia and a controlling headquarters established in the capital of Bosnia-Herzegovina, Sarajevo, to set up United Nations Protected Areas (UNPAs). These UNPAs covered the Krajina, Eastern Slavonia and Western Slavonia, and were divided up into four areas called Sectors East, North, South and West.

The situation that faced the first UNPROFOR commander, the Canadian General Lewis MacKenzie, on arrival at Sarajevo just as war had broken out in Bosnia-Herzegovina, typified the fatally delayed response of the UN throughout the wars. The source of the problem was the 'interpretation' of the mandates under which UN forces were operating – in other words, taken as being a purely humanitarian role in which the soldiers in blue helmets could only try and encourage peace, not enforce it. Neither the international community nor the Secretary General Boutros Boutros-Ghali wanted to use forceful methods to halt the killing. Britain, France and the United States did not want to accept the political, economic and military costs of becoming involved in a full-scale war in South East Europe. In the latter case, the Secretary General was adamant about explicitly using non-military means to

UNPROFOR
HELP US OR GO HOME

The frustration of ordinary citizens shown during a visit of the UN Secretary General about the slow response of the international community to end the fighting in Sarajevo in 1992. (ENRIQUE FOLGOSA/AFP via Getty Images)

resolve the crisis. Boutros Boutros-Ghali and his special envoy to the region, Yasushi Akashi, were major contributors to this 'soft' approach, which perhaps reflected the minimal consensus within the Security Council towards the wars in the former Yugoslavia. Consequently, these factors and preferred methods, when combined with the application of the traditional notions of peacekeeping – consent and impartiality – proved to be nothing short of disastrous for the inhabitants of the Balkans and for the reputation of the United Nations as a whole.

Theatre-based UNPROFOR commanders

As the fighting spread, so too did the UN commitment, swelling to over 30,000 personnel by 1994. Eventually, three UNPROFOR commands would be set up in Bosnia-Herzegovina, Croatia and Macedonia. Although an overarching UNPROFOR Force Commander was nominally in charge, the international media normally focused on the theatre-based UNPROFOR commander. In this respect, nations sent highly distinguished military leaders to the Balkans, but most were subsumed by the political nature of the task. General Philippe Morillon of France took over the UNPROFOR command in Bosnia-Herzegovina in September 1992, but had little success, and his tenure of command was notable for the assassination of the Deputy Prime Minister of Bosnia-Herzegovina, Hakija Turajlic, who was killed by a Bosnian Serb while surrounded by French soldiers in a French armoured personnel carrier in January 1993. His successor, the Belgian General Francis Briquemont (July 1993–January 1994), became renowned for spending his time largely around his headquarters in Sarajevo. In contrast, Britain sent a series of commanders who achieved varying degrees of success.

The first was General Sir Michael Rose (January 1994– January 1995), an unconventional soldier who had served primarily in the famed British Special Air Service (SAS) for most of his career. The appointment of General Rose was welcomed in many circles because it was widely felt that a tough soldier would resolve the problems. His unorthodox methods, such as walking down Sarajevo's sniper-infested streets without body armour, appeared to restore some confidence on the ground, and initial measures produced a limited ceasefire. Tragically, Bosniaks who emulated General Rose (as he encouraged them to do) would often wind up being shot dead by snipers who may have been reluctant to shoot the UN commander, but fellow citizens were quite another matter. Under Rose, an ardent supporter of the peacekeeping role, 'safe areas' set up to protect Bosnian Muslims from Bosnian Serb forces were tried, along with the collection of heavy weapons. But Rose's inability to deal firmly with the Bosnian Serbs meant that the fighting continued in the region. His successor, the less flamboyant General Sir Rupert Smith (January–December 1995), was perhaps the

most successful UN commander throughout the Balkan Wars. Considered by many to be one of the finest minds produced by the British Army during the Cold War, General Smith realised that the application of overwhelming force was the only means of getting the Serbs to stop 'spoiling', and take negotiations seriously. Under his command, and in concert with NATO forces, the bloodletting in Bosnia-Herzegovina was finally brought to a halt.

The UN soldier experience

Life for soldiers working for UNPROFOR was by no means easy. Dealing with thousands of refugees who were ethnically cleansed from all sides, Bosniaks, Bosnian Croats and Serbs, was especially difficult. At times, UN soldiers witnessed the process of ethnic cleansing as warring parties torched villages and destroyed normality. In Bosnia-Herzegovina alone millions of people were displaced by the fighting, and makeshift refugee camps would quickly descend into unhygienic and overcrowded areas full of hungry and desperate people. UN soldiers would also have to deal with the aftermath of massacres in which bodies of men, women and children would be found either shot, stabbed with knives, or in some cases burnt alive. Sometimes people would be killed in front of UN troops, who would stand by helplessly as the brutality and slaughter escalated. In addition, these deployments were not risk-free for the UN. Between 1992 and 1995, UN personnel were taken hostage, wounded, and in some cases killed (167 soldiers in total), either deliberately by snipers or caught in the open by mortars or artillery.

Occasionally, UN bases were deliberately targeted by the warring sides, not by just one or two shells but by dozens at a time. Apart from these physical dangers, UN soldiers also faced immense psychological trauma. For many European troops wearing blue helmets in the former Yugoslavia, the sight of people who looked just like them engaging in such inhuman acts was deeply disturbing. Nobody who saw at first hand the horrors of ethnic warfare in this region of Europe remained untouched in some way, whether realising it at the time, or when they returned home after their tour of duty was over.

LEFT
UN peacekeepers were often targeted by all sides. An injured French naval officer wounded by Bosnian Serb forces in Sarajevo pays his respect to a colleague killed during peacekeeping operations. (Photo by David Brauchli/ Getty Images)

All parties who became involved in the fighting in the former Yugoslavia, whether actively or passively, bear a great deal of responsibility for their actions or inactions and in this respect, the role of the United Nations can be heavily criticised despite the personal bravery of the soldiers on the ground trying to achieve the impossible. Undoubtedly, the thousands of humanitarian aid convoys escorted by the UN saved the lives of millions of people, but without decisive political and military action by the most powerful nations in the world to stop the fighting, these great deeds merely treated the symptoms of war, instead of tackling the root causes.

Bosnia-Herzegovina in flames

For a time it seemed that Bosnia-Herzegovina would escape the madness that had engulfed Croatia, as it contained the most mixed proportion of nationalities in the entire federation. Indeed, prior to the outbreak of war, Bosnia-Herzegovina was probably the most likely place in the Balkans where people would label themselves as 'Yugoslavs'. However, these cosmopolitan notions would be quickly shattered by the political ambitions and errors of key leaders, both regionally and internationally. It is well documented that Milosevic and Tudjman held a meeting in March 1991 at Karadjordjevo in Vojvodina, which included a discussion on the partition of Bosnia-Herzegovina between Croatia and Serbia, leaving the Bosniaks, who comprised the largest ethnic group in the country, with very little territory. Under this scheme, a Greater Croatia and a Greater Serbia would be carved out of what was formerly known as Bosnia-Herzegovina. In addition, as in Croatia, the JNA secretly armed the Bosnian Serbs from 1990 onwards, through a project known only by the letters 'RAM'.

The catalyst for war in Bosnia-Herzegovina can be traced to the international recognition of Croatia and Slovenia. Prior to this announcement, Bosnia-Herzegovena had tried

ABOVE Bosniak forces bloodied and wounded after an attack on Bosnian Serb positions around the city of Sarajevo. (Photo by Patrick Robert – Corbis/Sygma via Getty Images)

TOP The political leader of the Bosnian Serbs, Radovan Karadzic, with Arkan, the leader of the most notorious gang of paramilitaries. Karadzic is now serving a life sentence for war crimes and genocide. Arkan was shot dead in Belgrade in 2000. (BOZIDAR MILOSEVIC/AFP via Getty Images)

hard to chart a middle course between Croatia's desire for independence, and Serbian demands for the federation to remain intact.

Despite making strenuous protests to Helmut Kohl of Germany about the dangers of German foreign policy (in recognising the breakaway nations), the Bosniak President Izetbegovic suddenly decided to hold a referendum on independence on 1 March 1992, and it is perhaps no surprise that fighting began just a few weeks later.

Radovan Karadzic and Bosnian Serb tactics

Unlike Croatia in the first weeks of the war, Serbian strategy appeared more coherent and Serb forces made rapid progress in acquiring territory in Bosnia-Herzegovina. Perhaps the lessons of the fighting in the previous months had been absorbed, but the opposition was also substantially weaker. The Bosnian Serb leadership, like its counterpart in the Krajina, was made up of outlandish characters centred on the old tourist resort of Pale. The leader of the Bosnian Serbs was Radovan Karadzic, a man whose most noticeable feature was his unruly mane of white hair. His professional background, for a politician whose forces engaged in the most brutal ethnic cleansing, was surprising – he had been a psychiatrist in Sarajevo prior to the outbreak of war. Under Karadzic's political guidance, Bosnian Serb forces (who would eventually fall under the control of the irrepressible General Ratko Mladic) placed Sarajevo under a state of siege and terror for several years. Bosnian Serb tactics in the early stages of the fighting were simple and devastatingly effective in creating fear amongst millions of Bosniaks. Gangs of thugs, led by the likes of the Tigers and the White Eagles, would enter villages and towns, shooting people if necessary, to gain complete control of the area. Other forces would round up men to be detained in camps and jails (a few months later in the war, mass shootings were not uncommon) while the women and children would be separated from them. The most notorious of these camps was at Omarska, which contained approximately 5,000 detainees in the most appalling conditions. Often, people would

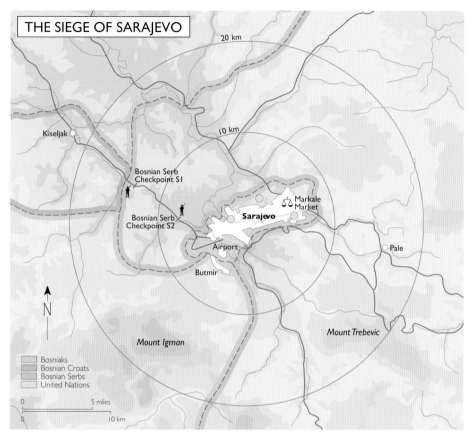

THE SIEGE OF SARAJEVO

Sarajevo was placed under siege by the Bosnian Serb forces on
the outlying hills, a strategy that was organised by the Bosnian Serb
leadership in the nearby resort of Pale. The 10km and 20km circles
around the city show the range of medium calibre and heavy calibre
mortars and guns.

be carrying out their daily lives, being at work, children at
school, when the criminal gangs would just roll into their
lives and normality would be turned upside down. Literally
within minutes, a lifetime of work, an investment in a career,
a marriage and a home would be rendered null and void by
Bosnian Serb forces encouraged to murder, loot and rape by
people like Milosevic and Karadzic, who seemed completely
detached from the misery. Why did neighbour turn so quickly

THE SIEGE OF SARAJEVO

It is extraordinary to think that a cosmopolitan city could be placed under a military siege in full gaze of the international community and turned into a terror-filled environment in which conducting daily life could be fatal. Sarajevo was effectively blockaded by the Bosnian Serb forces located on the outlying hills employing a strategy organised and directed by the Bosnian Serb leadership in the nearby resort of Pale. From this high ground, Bosnian Serb forces fired sniper rifles, heavy machine guns, mortars and heavy artillery at the unfortunate Bosniaks trapped in the city. People, usually civilians, were randomly shot dead on the streets and in their homes by snipers. Heavy weapons were ruthlessly fired into the city with inevitable consequences. The most notorious of these incidents were the infamous Markale Market massacres that occurred in 1994 and 1995, killing over 100 people. Getting out of Sarajevo was immensely difficult at this stage, and everyone – whether UN forces or civilians – had to cross two Bosnian Serb checkpoints (S1 and S2) on the main road out of the city towards Kiseljak. UN artillery units of the Rapid Reaction Force, based on Mount Igman, neutralised Bosnian Serb artillery positions during Operation *Deliberate Force* in 1995.

Fearfully crossing the road ('Sniper Alley', Sarajevo, 1994). Daily life in a city surrounded by snipers who deliberately targeted civilians. (Photo By Tom Stoddart Archive/Getty Images)

on neighbour? In part, due to the residual memory of the horrific events of World War II, but to a greater extent due to the unhealthy levels of propaganda spread by the Serbian political leadership about the Bosniaks and Bosnian Croats.

Bosniak political and military unpreparedness

Unlike the Bosnian Serbs, the Bosniaks were completely unprepared for the war, and this factor contributed to the rapid success of the Bosnian Serbs, whose area of territory extended to 70 per cent of Bosnia-Herzegovina and became known as Republika Srpska. The Bosniak President Izetbegovic, a lawyer by training and an Islamic scholar, was renowned for having written a thesis in 1973 which his enemies claimed called for an Islamic state to be established. This document, and Izetbegovic's radical views at the time, led to his imprisonment by the communist authorities on multiple occasions. At the start of the conflict, Izetbegovic was detained briefly by the JNA after returning from an international conference, and for much of the war he often isolated himself in Sarajevo. An intensely private man, Izetbegovic clearly struggled with the pressures of a war that some commentators claim was partly caused by his own actions with the referendum. Some of his other decisions, such as inviting Mujahideen to fight alongside his own forces, were also deeply questionable, particularly considering that the Bosnian Muslims were converted Slavs and practiced a very moderate form of Islam. Many of the radical Islamic fighters had a totally different outlook, one that moderate Muslims throughout the Islamic world considered extremist in every respect. Their presence on the battlefield merely added weight to the Serb propaganda that the Bosniaks were trying to set up a radical Islamic state. Likewise, Izetbegovic's subordinate, Vice-President Ejup Ganic, appeared completely out of his depth with the situation, manifesting itself when he broke down emotionally while giving a live radio interview, and some UN officials found him hard to take seriously. Only Haris Silajdzic, the Foreign Minister and later Prime Minister, was effective in getting across the plight of the Bosniaks to the outside world. These political weaknesses compounded the military unpreparedness of the Bosniaks in general, and the remaining 'Yugoslavs' in areas like Sarajevo. Consequently, much of the organisation of the fighting and defence was decentralised, and carried out to a significant extent by the criminal elements of Bosnia-Herzegovina. This would create other problems when the government eventually tried to reassert control at a later stage in the war. In one area, the so-called Bihac pocket, the government completely lost control

The fighting in BiH attracted many foreign fighters as volunteers, but the Mujahideen who came to fight for the Bosniaks developed a particularly poor reputation due to their sporadic brutality to civilians and aggressiveness towards UNPROFOR forces. (Photo by Pascal Le Segretain/Sygma via Getty Images)

to an enterprising businessman called Fikret Abdic, who managed to create an autonomous region by doing deals with all sides. In addition, Bosniak forces engaged in the same practices as their Bosnian Serbian counterparts when dealing with civilians and prisoners, and the Mujahideen gained an unsavoury reputation for ruthlessness.

The Bosnian Croat position

The Bosnian Croats were led eventually by Mate Boban (previously a supermarket manager), whose war aims were closely linked with Tudjman's vision to join the Bosnian Croatian territory – about 30 per cent of Bosnia-Herzegovina – with Croatia itself. To this end, on 5 July 1992 Boban declared the new Croat Union of Herceg-Bosna. This goal was quite different to that of the Bosniaks, who wanted to maintain the ethnic diversity of the nation under its traditional borders. Initially, the Bosnian Croats and Bosniaks formed a loose coalition against the Bosnian Serbs, but given that their war aims were quite different, it was inevitable that the union would break down. That said, the Bosnian Croat position was equally divided between Boban and the military branch (HOS) of the extreme right wing Croatian Party of Rights (HSP), which demanded more territory in Bosnia-Herzegovina. The leader of the HOS in western Herzegovina, Blaz Kraljevic, who had acquired an Australian accent having spent years working in that country, was shot to pieces in his car by Croatian Military Police (allegedly accidentally) using an anti-aircraft gun. Kraljevic's death had the effect of removing a competing power base from the Bosnian Croat political leadership. Nevertheless, the strategy and situation of the Bosnian Croats was quite different to their Bosniak allies. Firstly, much of their territory bordered Croatia, and a great deal of the fighting was done by the Croatian Army (HV), despite claims that it was just the Bosnian Croats (HVO) carrying out the operations. Like their Bosnian Serb counterparts, Bosnian Croats were not immune

ABOVE For a time Bosnian Croat forces and Bosniaks worked together in a loose affiliation against the Bosnian Serbs. Here Bosniak fighters working in concert with Bosnian Croat forces pull out of Jajce in 1992. (PATRICK BAZ/AFP via Getty Images)

to practising ethnic cleansing, looting, and the widespread rape of captured women.

The failure of international diplomacy

The inability of the international community to halt the bloodshed in the Balkans must rank as one of the most damning indictments of the structures and mechanisms of the world order since the Munich Agreement of 1938. The European Community initially sent military monitors (ECMM) to try to verify who the aggressors were, and appointed high-level diplomats such as Lord Carrington and later Lord Owen to try to resolve the crises.

The Vance-Owen Peace Plan

Lord Owen and his UN counterpart, Cyrus Vance, put together a controversial proposal to end the fighting in Bosnia-Herzegovina in late 1992, called the Vance-Owen Peace Plan (VOPP).

This plan basically divided the country into ten areas, or cantons, along ethnic lines, with control being shared by all parties (with the exception of Sarajevo). In the bulk of the literature on the collapse of the former Yugoslavia, the VOPP is universally criticised, though a few notable writers, like Misha Glenny, do emphasise its merits. Part of the problem with the VOPP was that, despite forcing the Serbs to hand back about 25 per cent of their annexed territory, it was also a recognition that the situation had fundamentally changed in the country, and the new political reality needed to be addressed. For some, this was merely rewarding Bosnian

BELOW The international negotiators Lord David Owen (left) and Cyrus Vance (right) lay the foundation for their plan to bring peace in 1993. (HAIDO/AFP via Getty Images)

ABOVE From late 1992 onwards, the Vance-Owen Peace Plan was an attempt to end the fighting by broadly accepting the new reality on the ground in Bosnia-Herzegovina.

Serb and Serbian aggression and dealing with their leaders as legitimate parties in a dispute, rather than as criminals who had created the chaos in the first place.

In this respect, international diplomacy was morally bankrupt in its willingness to negotiate with people who actively encouraged and armed people to murder, loot and rape. But given that the international community was unwilling to use decisive force to stop the fighting, then clearly accommodation with all of the parties was viewed as the only way forward.

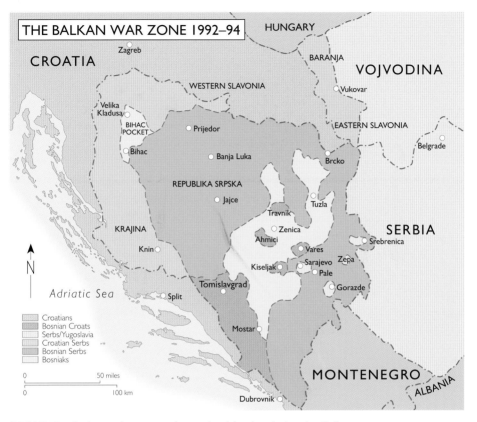

THE BALKAN WAR ZONE 1992–94

CROATIA

HUNGARY

Zagreb

BARANJA

VOJVODINA

WESTERN SLAVONIA

Vukovar

Velika
Kladusa

BIHAC
POCKET

Prijedor

EASTERN SLAVONIA

Belgrade

Bihac

Banja Luka

Brcko

REPUBLIKA SRPSKA

Jajce

Tuzla

Travnik

KRAJINA

Zenica

SERBIA

Ahmici

Srebrenica

Knin

Vares

N

Kiseljak

Sarajevo   Zepa

Pale

Adriatic Sea

Tomislavgrad

Gorazde

Split

Croatians
Bosnian Croats
Serbs/Yugoslavia
Croatian Serbs
Bosnian Serbs
Bosniaks

Mostar

0   50 miles

0   100 km

MONTENEGRO

ALBANIA

Dubrovnik

ABOVE The Serbs made spectacular territorial gains during the Balkan Wars, from setting up the Krajina and seizing the key provinces of Eastern and Western Slavonia in Croatia, to grasping vast swathes of land in Bosnia-Herzegovina.

The three parties perceived the VOPP in very different ways. The Bosnian Croats were happy with the scheme, as it fulfilled most of their ambitions. In contrast, the Bosniaks stood to lose the most from this acceptance of the situation on the ground, and the Bosnian Serbs also lost key territory that they had taken through force of arms. Unfortunately, however, when the Bosnian Croats tried to implement the VOPP in their areas the following year, it pushed the already fragile relationship with their allies to breaking point, and war broke out between them. In the final analysis, the Vance-Owen Peace Plan was a diplomatic disaster.

Conflict of international aims

A major source of the disharmony within the international community was the conflict of aims between the major world powers in dealing with the Balkan problem. The British, who held the EU Presidency at a critical time during the first year of the war, were most reluctant to get heavily involved in a military sense.

The British position that was strongly held by Prime Minister John Major and Foreign Secretary Douglas Hurd placed a heavy emphasis on peacekeeping forces. Their rejection of a forceful response in the early years of the crises led some writers to condemn their policies as being a significant contributory factor in the continuation of the slaughter, by virtue of the fact that their diplomacy made it difficult for other European nations and NATO to take more decisive action. The shifting position of the United States was another major element in the failure of the international order to stop the disintegration of the former Yugoslavia.

Unfortunately, as events unfolded in the Balkans between 1990 and 1991, the attention of the United States was firmly on the Middle East and the outbreak of the Gulf War. Furthermore, the run-up to the presidential election between 1991 and 1992 meant that America's focus was for a critical time on the domestic agenda. In addition, President George Bush's key diplomats in relation to the area – the US ambassador to Yugoslavia, Walter Zimmermann, and Lawrence Eagleburger of the State Department – were slow to push for a firm line against Milosevic until 1992, and consequently the US signals to the region and all sides were mixed at best. Only President Clinton, and the appointment of the US diplomat Richard Holbrooke in 1995, brought about a resolution to the problem, and even then it took two years for US strategy to become truly effective.

The Bosniak-Croat Civil War 1993–94

The outbreak of the Bosniak-Croat Civil War in the spring of 1993 added a further level of complexity to the situation in Bosnia-Herzegovina. The issue of Bosniak refugees fleeing southwards away from the Bosnian Serb onslaught around Banja Luka, towards Bosnian Croat areas such as Travnik had been causing tensions between the two sides long before sporadic fighting broke out in January 1993.

Croatia was supporting nearly 300,000 refugees during this period, and inevitably this social burden, allied with a desire by the Bosnian Croats to start asserting their political ambitions in areas that had been considered part of Bosnia-Herzegovina, created a highly flammable situation. For the British contingent of UNPROFOR, the fighting around Gornji Vakuf between the Croats and the Bosniaks led to their first fatality. Lance-Corporal Wayne Edwards was shot through the right cheek while driving a Warrior vehicle that was escorting an ambulance into Gornji Vakuf. His death was not an accident – several of the white-painted Warriors had been hit by single shots just prior to the fatal shot. Clearly the UN forces had been deliberately targeted.

For a few months the fighting died down and simmered, before breaking out on a much larger scale in April 1993. Most historians are in agreement that the violent kidnapping of the local Bosnian Croat commander Zivko Totic in Zenica on 15 April was the cause of the renewed outbreak of violence. Totic's car was held up, and four of his bodyguards, along with a pedestrian, were shot dead on the spot before Totic was bundled into another vehicle and driven away. Fighting then broke out on a large scale in Vitez. The conflict between the erstwhile allies concentrated initially around the strategically significant Lasva valley in central Bosnia, which contained valuable munitions factories including Vitez and Travnik. The designated capital of the Bosnian-Croat entity, Mostar, which demographically contained more Bosniaks than Croats prior to the fighting, became a household name across the world due to the amount of media coverage of the bloody fighting between the two sides. Interestingly, the Bosnian Croats came out of the fighting in a worse state, not only in terms of international reputation, but also in a military sense.

The massacre at Ahmici

Several incidents condemned the Croatian forces in the eyes of the world community. The first was the massacre of Bosniak civilians in the village of Ahmici, discovered by British UN forces on 22 April 1993. A few days earlier, the village had been attacked by a special Croatian anti-terrorist unit called the 'Jokers', along with some military policemen, about 75 men in total.

A recent account of this attack has tried to justify it as a deliberate spoiling assault, to pre-empt Muslim forces launching an offensive. However, this legitimisation of the violence is still undermined by the horrific events in the village. People were systematically dragged out of their houses. First the men were shot, then the male children, and

BELOW
Remembering the victims of the 1993 Ahmici massacre in 2020. (Photo by Haris Badzic/ Anadolu Agency via Getty Images)

finally the females. The Croatian forces had located snipers on the edges of the village so that anyone trying to escape would be cut down before they reached safety. Every living thing, from humans to pets, was killed by the Croatian forces that morning. After the slaughter, the bodies were thrown into the houses and set alight with petrol. The British soldiers found 104 bodies in the remains of the houses, many of them burnt beyond recognition, and strewn across the village were the corpses of bloated animals, from horses to dogs. It was a ghastly scene, and one of the worst examples of ethnic cleansing in the fighting.

ABOVE The tragedy of Mostar and its famous bridge. The fighting was between the Bosnian Croats and the Bosniaks. (Roger Hutchings/In Pictures Ltd./Corbis via Getty Images)

The Convoy of Joy and the Mostar bridge

A few months later, in June, Croatian forces attacked a humanitarian aid convoy known as the 'Convoy of Joy', which was taking much-needed supplies to starving Bosniaks. Under the gaze of UN forces, the Croats murdered several of the truck drivers and then Croatian refugees started to loot the vehicles whilst being filmed by the international media. Later that year, on 9 November, Croatian forces also deliberately targeted the medieval bridge in Mostar and destroyed it with heavy artillery.

For a continent that had suffered the horrors of deliberate cultural bombing under Hitler's Third Reich, the destruction of the bridge at Mostar represented a new low in Europe's history. Ethnic cleansing and murder were committed by both sides in the civil war, but these notable incidents gained the most international news coverage, which ultimately swung world opinion against the Croatians.

Co-operation between enemies

Militarily speaking, the war with the Bosniaks was a catastrophe for the Bosnian Croats. They lost enormous amounts of territory in Central Bosnia, such as the capture of Travnik in early June, which cost them an estimated 250 dead and created some 15,000 refugees. This pattern continued south of Travnik, as the Bosnian Croats lost village after village to the advancing Bosniak forces, creating tens of thousands of refugees that fled either to Croatia or across into Serb-controlled areas where the men would be put in camps. The Bosnian Serbs were clearly the winners in the fighting, and were happy to help their neighbours kill each other. It has been reported that Serb artillery fired in support of the Bosniak forces around Gornji Vakuf when they discovered that the latter had run out of ammunition. Deals would be struck by local commanders on different sides regarding heavy artillery support. These unhealthy levels of cooperation between enemies, who would in a heartbeat try to kill each other, mystified outside observers, who were quick to forget that these people had been neighbours long before the fighting.

The war between the two sides ended in late February 1994. Enormous diplomatic pressure from the United States, in combination with the weakened state of both protagonists in Bosnia-Herzegovina, resulted in the formation of a new Bosniak-Croat Federation.

Safe areas

With the general unwillingness of some senior UN commanders to interpret the peacekeeping mandate in a more robust fashion, it was immensely difficult to persuade the three sides to stop fighting. The nub of the problem was how to halt the use of heavy weapons. This was eventually resolved by the gradual involvement of NATO in the region.

NATO involvement

In July 1992, NATO members agreed that the alliance could be used for operations in the Balkans, and by October NATO was enforcing the 'no-fly zone' over Bosnia-Herzegovina. After all, Serbia possessed a significant quantity of multi-role aircraft as well as helicopters, and this was a means of preventing them from being used in a punitive sense against the Croats and the Bosniaks. In February 1994, the organisation created in 1949 to protect Western Europe against the Soviet Union fired its first shots in anger, when NATO warplanes shot down four Serb aircraft violating the no-fly zone over Banja Luka. In the summer of the following year, an American plane patrolling over Bihac was shot down by Serb forces, and its pilot, Scott O'Grady, spent a week hiding from the pursuing Serb forces before being rescued by the US military. The success of the air patrols was mixed at best, and official sources reveal that over 400 violations of the no-fly zone occurred between 1992 and 1993 by all three sides. At sea off the Adriatic coast, NATO warships were engaged in Operation *Sharp Guard* to enforce the UN arms embargo on the former Yugoslavia by intercepting arms smugglers.

Dual-track international policy

To try to stop the horrors that were occurring on a daily basis on the ground, the international community adopted a dual-track policy that combined legal and military options. In order to prosecute those who had been involved in the ethnic

cleansing, and to deter others who might consider engaging in such activities, a war crimes tribunal was set up at The Hague. The remit of this body was to gather evidence on alleged war criminals in order to bring them to trial. In Bosnia-Herzegovina from early 1993 onwards, the UN created the six so-called 'safe areas' around Bihac, Gorazde, Srebrenica, Sarajevo, Tuzla and Zepa, to protect the Muslims from the advancing Bosnian Serb forces. In addition, the adoption of a robust resolution (UNSCR 836) allowed UNPROFOR to enforce the mandate with 'all necessary measures' – including air strikes – though the words 'protect' and 'defend' were deliberately left out of this resolution. After the passing of the resolution, the UN Secretariat recommended that an extra 32,000 soldiers would be needed to make the 'safe area' policy work. However, the British, in particular, were strongly opposed to this new proposal. A French plan that called for a lighter option of 5,000 troops was the 'preferred' approach. Like the no-fly zone, this represented a concrete yet substantially watered-down measure by the international community to draw a line in the sand concerning Serbian aggression in Bosnia-Herzegovina. Any infringement of a safe area would incur a NATO military response using air power. These UN-sanctioned missions were given the title 'Blue Sword' close air support strikes. On paper, this set-up should have worked to deter, if not halt, any aggression by Bosnian Serb forces towards the safe areas, but in fact it failed miserably for a number of reasons. The command and control element of the strikes was elaborate, and relied on a dual key approach whereby NATO needed UN approval to initiate air strikes. In theory, this arrangement required several critical steps to be taken before orders could be translated into action – the verification of a Bosnian Serb violation of a safe area would be passed to the UN commander in Sarajevo, who would make a judgement call as to whether it merited a military response. If so, a request would be placed with the UN's

OPPOSITE US Marines on USS *Kearsarge* ready themselves to rescue Scott O'Grady, whose F-16 was shot down by Serb forces. (Photo by Peter Turnley/Corbis/VCG via Getty Images)

Special Representative, Yasushi Akashi, who would consult with the UN Headquarters and Boutros-Ghali. If all parties agreed then the request would be passed to the NATO chain of command, and the bombing missions initiated. At best this was convoluted, at worst it offered too many opportunities for interested parties to delay or even prevent swift action. Official figures suggest that the vast majority of UN fatalities (117 in total) occurred in and around these 'safe' areas, in addition to up to 20,000 civilian deaths.

Gorazde

Events in Gorazde in April 1994 can be viewed as a case study of the failure of the safe areas policy. When the Bosnian Serbs starting attacking the town the UN response was extremely limited – just a couple of air strikes were attempted. General Sir Michael Rose actually sent a team of British Special Forces to the town, to verify reports by a party of United Nations Military Observers (UNMOs) that the safe area was being violated. The Special Forces suffered a fatality (Corporal Fergus Rennie, killed deliberately by the Bosnian Serbs) and another soldier seriously wounded while they were trying to gather accurate information. Although they radioed to Sarajevo about the desperate situation, the UN command staff refused to believe them. One historian suggests that General Rose had an interest in downplaying the reports of both the UNMOs and his own Special Forces team that Gorazde was about to fall to the Bosnian Serbs, as it contradicted his own personal belief that the Bosniaks had concocted the whole thing to bring the international community into the war. This entire incident was further recorded in the memoirs of the Royal Navy pilot Lt Nick Richardson, whose Sea Harrier was shot down over Gorazde whilst trying to carry out an air strike, and who managed to join the SAS team in the town. Other accounts suggest that, despite persuading their headquarters in Sarajevo that the safe area was about to fall, the Special Forces were advised to surrender to the Bosnian Serbs, with the hope that in a few months the UN would get them released. The SAS and Lt Richardson very sensibly declined this option, and eventually managed to persuade General Rose to arrange a helicopter extraction once they had crossed Bosnian Serb lines at night, carrying their wounded colleague. A more robust response at Gorazde could possibly have stopped the Bosnian Serb aggression in its tracks, and then perhaps a negotiated settlement could have been achieved in 1994, instead of a year later.

Bihac

In the Bihac pocket, another safe area, a bizarre situation developed from late 1993 onwards. Bosniak forces loyal to the government started fighting with forces loyal to the rogue Bosniak businessman Fikret Abdic. By August 1994, the government forces had won the internal battle and wrested control of Bihac from Abdic, who fled into Croatia. Two months later, it was the Bosniaks who initiated hostilities with the Bosnian Serbs, as the Fifth Corps launched an all-out assault southwards from Bihac and briefly recaptured a vast expanse of territory. This attack put UNPROFOR and the international community in a very difficult position, especially when the Bosnian Serbs initiated a successful counter-attack in November, which quickly pushed the Bosniaks back into the Bihac pocket. The problem for the UN was how to stop the Bosnian Serbs from crossing into the safe area, and ultimately the response was, once more, very limited air strikes. The crisis over Bihac revealed the deep divisions within the UN regarding how to deal with the Bosnian Serbs. Many members called for a punitive campaign that would stop them completely, but in order for NATO to achieve this aim Bosnian Serb air defences would have to be neutralised, and General Rose (and many contributing nations to the peacekeeping effort) was deeply opposed to

NEXT PAGES
A typical Bosnian Serb siege position dominating the high ground around Gorazde in 1994. (Photo by Pool MERILLON/ SHONE/Gamma-Rapho via Getty Images)

UNPROFOR AND SAFE AREAS IN BOSNIA–HERZEGOVINA

CROATIA

Zagreb ◯ UN HQ
Force Commander

HUNGARY

UNPA
SECTOR EAST

UNPA
SECTOR WEST

UNPA
SECTOR NORTH

VOJVODINA

Vukovar
Russian Forces

Bihac
Bangladeshi Forces

Brcko

UNPA
SECTOR SOUTH

BOSNIA-HERZEGOVINA

Tuzla

SERBIA

Vitez
British Forces

Knin ◯

UN HQ ◯ Vares
Kiseljak

Srebrenica
Zepa ◯ Dutch Forces

Gornji Vakuf ◯

Sarajevo
UN HQ
Canadian Forces
French Forces

Gorazde

Tomislavgrad ◯

Adriatic Sea
Operation *Sharp Guard*

◯ Split

Mostar ◯ Spanish
Forces

N

MONTENEGRO

ALBANIA

▭ United Nations presence

0   50 miles
0   100 km

The initial deployment of UN forces in Croatia, known as UNPROFOR 1, was concentrated in the so-called United Nations Protected Areas (UNPAs), which were divided into four sectors: North, South, East and West.

UNPROFOR being dragged into a war by these NATO actions. Consequently, these divisions, and the inability of the limited air strikes to have any serious effect, merely encouraged the Bosnian Serb forces to keep pursuing their political objectives by military means.

By spring 1995, the situation was rapidly breaking down on the ground in Bosnia-Herzegovina, especially with the failure of General Rose's much-vaunted Cessation of

Hostilities Agreement (COHA), signed in December 1994 between the Bosniaks and the Bosnian Serbs. Interestingly, the appointment of a new UNPROFOR commander, General Rupert Smith, created even more divisions within the UN hierarchy in the former Yugoslavia, due to Smith's desire for a much stronger military response to Bosnian Serb aggression. This view contrasted sharply with those of the UN's Special Representative, Yasushi Akashi, and the overall Force Commander, General Bernard Janvier, who were reluctant to allow UN forces to be dragged into the conflict. Consequently, the limited air strike option merely encouraged the Bosnian Serbs to adopt a new tactic of taking UN forces hostage as human shields. By 26 May, approximately 400 UN personnel were either taken hostage or prevented from moving by Bosnian Serb forces, and in one incident a day later, two French UN soldiers were killed trying to recapture a UN position that had been seized by Bosnian Serb forces. Eventually, through intense diplomatic negotiations, the hostages were released, but the lesson was quite clear that, in the light of the UN inability to take decisive action against the Bosnian Serb forces, all the lightly armed UN units scattered throughout the 'safe areas' were seriously vulnerable to becoming hostages. The limited numbers of UN forces in these areas also meant that they were often heavily outnumbered. Put simply, the soldiers on the ground in the former Yugoslavia had been put in an impossible position by squabbling diplomats (and their national interests), a situation that would become painfully obvious in the summer.

Srebrenica

By June 1995, the situation had badly deteriorated and the fighting had substantially intensified, so much so that the UN was seriously considering the option of withdrawal of its peacekeeping forces from the region. Other options included bolstering the UN forces with a 'rapid reaction force or theatre reserve', which was eventually deployed. However, great divisions existed about how these additional forces should be used. In a letter sent to Radovan Karadzic on 19 June, the UN's Special Representative, Yasushi Akashi, went out of his way to assure the Bosnian Serb leadership that these additional forces would not alter the nature of the UN's peacekeeping forces. The upshot of these highly mixed signals (sending additional forces but with reassurances) was that the Bosnian Serbs were not deterred in any significant way from pursuing their own ends with regard to the safe areas. In Srebrenica, a small detachment of Dutch peacekeepers called Dutchbat 3 (Dutch battalion) was given responsibility for the safe area from January 1995 onwards. On paper the Dutch battalion, under the command of Lt Col. Thom Karremans, was 600 strong, but in fact only half these numbers were actual fighting soldiers.

Dutchbat 3 was armed with armoured personnel carriers with heavy machine guns, a TOW (Tube-launched, Optically tracked, Wire-guided) missile launcher, and, of course, their personal weapons. Overall, a very lightly armed force in comparison with the estimated 1,000–2,000 Bosnian Serbs of the Fifth 'Drina' Corps, which possessed tanks, APCs and supporting artillery. In contrast, the Bosniak forces of the Twenty-Eighth Division, with around 4,000 soldiers, had no heavy weapons apart from light mortars and a few anti-tank missiles. The overall impression was of the Bosnian Serbs possessing a qualitative superiority over the more numerous Bosniaks, not only in terms of heavy weapons but also in training. The sporadic fighting in and around Srebrenica took a new twist on 3 June 1995, when a Bosnian Serb raid actually targeted one of Dutchbat 3's observation posts (OP Echo). Calls by Colonel Karremans for air support to save his men were denied, the OP was captured, and more UN hostages fell into Bosnian Serb hands. The situation in

Srebrenica had, in fact, been getting worse for months, and Colonel Karremans had repeatedly requested assistance from the UN, but with little success given the problems occurring throughout Bosnia-Herzegovina at the same time. The low priority of Srebrenica meant that by June, Dutchbat 3 and the inhabitants of Srebrenica were running low on fuel, food and manpower – at least 150 of Colonel Karremans' men had been prevented from rejoining the unit in the town. UN intelligence assessments indicated that, although the situation was bad in Srebrenica, it was unlikely to be the focus of the Bosnian Serb strategy, since attacks in other areas appeared stronger and more frequent.

The main attack on Srebrenica occurred on 6 July, with the Bosnian Serbs using both tanks and heavy artillery to reduce strong-points and soften up the defenders. The Dutch peacekeepers, on realising the nature of the assault, called for air support as the fighting got closer to their observation posts. Unfortunately, General Smith was away on leave (quite a common practice as even top commanders require a break away from the enormous stress) and therefore much of the crisis was dealt with by the overall Force Commander General Janvier and his staff in Zagreb, and Smith's multinational deputies in Sarajevo. The initial Dutch request for support was refused, but the Bosnian Serbs surprisingly halted their attack the next day. The attack resumed on 8 July, one day after General Mladic and President Milosevic had met with the EU Representative, Carl Bildt, to discuss the resumption of the peace process! Again, on the ground in Srebrenica, the fighting began to move towards the Dutch observation positions, and close air support was once more requested but ruled out by UN commanders in Zagreb. Soon another observation post, OP Foxtrot, was overrun, and the UN forces manning it withdrew. One Dutch soldier was killed in this process, by Bosniak fighters as they drove through a roadblock in order to retreat from the advancing

Dutch UN soldiers in conversation with Bosniak fighters in March 1994. By July 1995, this unit of soldiers would be embroiled in the worst act of genocide in Europe since the end of World War II: the Srebrenica massacre. (ED OUDENAARDEN/AFP via Getty Images)

Bosnian Serb forces. Another UN position, OP Uniform, was also surrounded and the Dutch soldiers were taken hostage. The next day, the Bosnian Serb advance continued in the same manner – attacking UN positions and rolling up the pocket bit by bit. For the Dutchbat commander in Srebrenica, UNPROFOR's strategy of threatening air strikes but then relenting at the last minute put him and his soldiers in a desperate position. They tried warning off the Bosnian Serbs with mortar-fired flares and heavy machine-gun fire over the heads of the Serbs, but these measures were in vain. On 11 July, with the Bosnian Serbs on the outskirts of Srebrenica, Colonel Karremans had been convinced by an order from UNPROFOR that massive air strikes were on the way that morning. However, all that appeared in reality was two bombs dropped by NATO warplanes that overflew Srebrenica. The two bombs merely incensed the Bosnian Serb forces, led openly at this stage by General Mladic, who started threatening the lives of the captured Dutch peacekeepers. In the early hours of the next day, a ceasefire was arranged between the remainder of the Bosniaks, many of whom were crowded into the Dutch compound in their thousands, and the Bosnian Serb Army. The official report suggests that confusion in the UNPROFOR chain of command was the source of the misunderstanding over the air strikes.

The massacre at Srebrenica

The events that occurred in the aftermath of the 'surrender' of the safe area of Srebrenica will haunt the international community and those leaders in the UN and UNPROFOR for decades. The remaining Bosniak fighters tried to break through Bosnian Serb lines, but many were cut down by machine-gun fire and the alleged use of non-lethal chemical weapons. For the remaining population of Srebrenica, the men and older boys were separated from the women and children, in some cases with the assistance of UN representatives. The women and children were taken by bus out of Srebrenica towards Bosniak territory, and the men and boys were taken elsewhere. It is estimated that 8,000 males of various ages were executed in the following days by Bosnian Serb forces, despite General Mladic telling all the refugees (filmed by the international media) that they would not be harmed. Most, it seems, were driven to remote locations where they were simply shot dead. Witnesses to the massacres recount tales of how even the bus drivers were forced to take part in the killings, so that all were implicated in the dreadful acts of murder. For the

The process of uncovering war crimes. Investigators carefully excavate a mass grave site near Pilica in 1996 in Bosnian Serb-controlled territory. Some mass graves were dumping sites for bodies killed elsewhere whereas others were execution sites as well. (ODD ANDERSEN/AFP via Getty Images)

UN, the whole incident was, and remains today, one of the most indelible stains on its credibility, and seven years later a report by the Dutch government into the massacre led to the mass resignation of that administration. The key lesson from Srebrenica was that treating war criminals, thugs and plain murderers, like General Mladic and President Milosevic, with moral equivalence and respect in relation to the other parties in the Balkans, was a recipe for genocide on a mass scale.

THE WORLD AROUND WAR

Global perspectives

The outbreak of fighting in the former Yugoslavia occurred at a time when the structure of international society was changing rapidly. With the end of the Cold War, western nations, in particular, were keen to reap the benefits of the new climate, and reduce the massive amounts of defence spending that had characterised the superpower rivalry for over 40 years. The Gulf War of 1991 appeared to be the exception to this trend, but in many ways the economic benefits of liberating Kuwait and bolstering the security of Saudi Arabia, two of the world's most significant oil-producing countries, far outweighed the financial outlay on military forces. Indeed, despite the United States providing the bulk of the fighting forces, the overall cost of the Gulf War was shouldered by other members of the coalition. In contrast, military involvement in the Balkans offered little in the way of economic benefits that would appeal to the petrol-driven economies of Europe and the United States. Instead, enhanced military involvement would be a 'sunk cost', borne by the taxpayers who had just been promised reduced defence expenditure. In addition, and above all other considerations, any commitment to the region – given the levels of division – would be a long-term proposition. For nations like Britain, which had spent the last 20 years trying to resolve armed conflict between various factions of Catholics and Protestants in Northern Ireland, the experience of throwing money and lives (civilian and military) into such a scenario was painfully familiar. However, a direct comparison with Northern Ireland in terms of causes of the violence, though ostensibly similar, is in fact a completely false analogy. In the Balkans it was a state (Serbia) that was causing the violence, and its powers in terms of money and disposable military forces were in a different league to the ragtag terrorist organisations in Northern Ireland, which managed to smuggle in a few rifles or pounds of explosive on an occasional basis.

The reluctance to engage in more robust humanitarian missions was not confined to South East Europe. In 1993, the United States suffered the loss of 18 Special Operations Forces or SOF (Rangers and Delta Force) in a disastrous incident in Somalia that was subsequently immortalised by the movie *Black Hawk Down*. The sight of dead American servicemen being dragged through the streets of Mogadishu by a howling mob of Somalis, relayed around the world by the international news media, was enough to persuade President Bill Clinton to withdraw US forces from the peacekeeping mission. Clearly, although Operation *Desert Storm* in Kuwait had managed to banish some of the ghosts of Vietnam, the dreadful events in Somalia revealed that the United States was still very sensitive to casualties. Indeed, the word 'Somalia' became a mantra to those sceptics who did not want to actively end the fighting in the former Yugoslavia. Furthermore, the early 1990s were overshadowed by yet another example of the reluctance of the international community to intervene and stop ethnic fighting, this time in Africa. In 1994, hostilities broke out between the Hutu and Tutsi tribes in Rwanda, and within a matter of months approximately 800,000 people were killed, largely with machetes, in one of the most horrific examples of genocide in modern memory. Neither the United Nations nor the most powerful nations in the world moved quickly to try to stop the

OPPOSITE An example of the iconic Black Hawk helicopter flying over Mogadishu, Somalia in 1993. (Photo by Scott Peterson/Liaison/ Getty Images)

bloodletting, and once more global citizens were abandoned by the very institutions set up to prevent such tragedies. For cynics, the pattern of international relations in the early to mid-1990s seemed to indicate that powerful states would only intervene decisively in conflicts when their own political and economic interests were threatened; otherwise the attitude was one of laissez faire with minimal involvement.

Spill-over

The fighting in the former Yugoslavia had significant consequences for neighbouring countries in terms of security. The buzz-word of the early 1990s was 'spill-over' – in other words, the fear that the fighting might spread to other countries and develop into a much bigger conflagration. Consequently, with this concern in mind and responding to a personal request from the Macedonian President, UNSCR 795 was passed on 11 December 1992, and saw the deployment of a small UNPROFOR unit to Macedonia, with its headquarters in Skopje, to monitor Macedonia's borders with Serbia and Montenegro as well as Albania. There was also a great danger that the Balkan 'tinderbox' could actually inflame an already tense relationship in the region between two NATO allies, Greece and Turkey. Throughout the 1990s, relations between these two countries had worsened, with much of the tension stemming from the division of Cyprus in 1974. Greek and Turkish warplanes would often engage in dogfights or air combat manoeuvring while on patrol over the Aegean Sea, with the potential for escalation into much greater levels of hostility. The connection with the Balkans stemmed from Greece's longstanding dispute over the status of Macedonia, and good links politically and culturally with Serbia. Slobodan Milosevic and his family actually owned holiday properties in the Greek Islands. Turkey, the modern name for the nation that had once been the wellspring of the

Ottoman Empire, inevitably felt greater sympathy for fellow Muslims in Yugoslavia who were clearly being persecuted by Orthodox Christians. The scope for a much wider conflict in South East Europe seemed like a not-too-far-fetched idea in the early 1990s.

The refugee crisis

Like all wars and conflicts, the killing and general chaos in the former Yugoslavia created millions of refugees, who, quite naturally, tried to get away from the rising tide of violence. The United Nations High Commissioner for Refugees (UNHCR) was the lead agency for dealing with this tidal wave of humanity, characterised by people fleeing their homes with few belongings apart from what they could carry. In Bosnia-Herzegovina it has been estimated that, of the original 4.4 million people living in the country prior to the outbreak of war, over half were forced out of their homes and had to move elsewhere. In addition, over a million left the country entirely and resettled abroad, with around 50 per cent going to Germany. Refugees headed not only for Western Europe, but also across the Atlantic Ocean to North America. Initially, widespread sympathy existed for the displaced populations, but over time, as the conflicts dragged on, the refugees became an increasing economic burden to those nations who had offered hospitality. In Britain, for example, tension flared up around the ports of South East England, between refugees at reception points and local communities, as both sides competed for scarce jobs. Refugees also brought with them their own cultures, and inevitably faced problems trying to adapt to countries with a completely different set of norms and values, as well as language. The failure to resolve the Balkan problem proved to be not just a political and security issue, but also an increasingly significant financial burden for the international community.

As 'UN-protected' safe areas were captured, thousands of people were ordered to leave their homes by the Bosnian Serb forces and ended up as refugees, such as the inhabitants of Zepa. (Photo by Patrick Robert – Corbis/Sygma via Getty Images)

The United States

The position of the United States in the collapse of the former Yugoslavia was perhaps the most ambiguous of all the nations watching the horrors unfold. Clearly the US had the most disposable military power of all the states in the world, yet it chose to remain on the sidelines for much of the initial diplomacy. At an individual level, however, Americans were at the heart of UN diplomacy to end the bloodshed. Cyrus Vance, the former Secretary of State under President Carter and a man with a wealth of diplomatic experience, was appointed as the Personal Envoy of Secretary General Javier Perez de Cuellar, to try to resolve the conflict. His 'Vance Plan' ensured the deployment of the first UN peacekeepers to Croatia, a move that would later be extended to Bosnia-Herzegovina. As the fighting continued in 1993, Secretary of State Warren Christopher proposed a plan called 'Lift and Strike' to halt Serb aggression. Put simply, lift the arms embargo, rearm the Bosniaks, and at the same time use NATO air power to threaten strikes against the Bosnian Serbs. European nations such as Britain were deeply opposed to such a move, as they felt it would widen the conflict. Nevertheless, despite facing immense opposition from their European counterparts, the United States under Bill Clinton did try to resolve the imbalance of military forces on the ground by using quite unorthodox methods. In the first instance, an American private military company called Military Professional Resources Incorporated (MPRI) started to train the Croatian Army into an effective fighting force. The management board of MPRI contained extremely senior, yet retired, members of the US Army, which suggests that their links with the US administration were significant. Secondly, alongside the food aid flights dropping 'Meals Ready to Eat' (MRE) to starving Bosniaks on the ground, there is credible evidence to suggest that the United States was secretly smuggling weapons to the Bosniaks, using transport aircraft landing at night in places like Tuzla, while fighter escorts made a great deal of noise to detract attention from these blacked-out aircraft. From 1994 onwards, US policy was visibly represented on the ground by two key people: Assistant Secretary of State for European Affairs Richard Holbrooke, and General Wesley Clark, who would become Supreme Allied Commander, Europe (SACEUR), NATO's highest commander, in 1997. Both men would also play an instrumental role in NATO's forceful response to Serbia's policies in Kosovo in 1999.

General Wesley
Clark, NATO's
Supreme
Commander, gives a
television interview
during Operation
Allied Force in
Kosovo in 1999.
(Photo By NATO/
Getty Images)

NATO

The end of the Cold War and the disintegration of Yugoslavia into armed conflict propelled NATO into the limelight. Great question marks hung over the future of the organisation that had ensured Europe's security since its inception in 1949. In the early 1990s, many commentators were openly speculating about the ongoing role of the North Atlantic Treaty Organisation. On the one hand, people argued that it had fulfilled its purpose, and as a Cold War structure it was out of place in the new world order. This position was reinforced by an American perspective which stressed that the United States had done enough for Europe, and it was now time to bring the troops home. On the other hand, it was suggested that the end of the Cold War represented a new opportunity for NATO to expand into areas previously controlled by the Soviet Union in Eastern Europe. After all, it was the premier security organisation in the world, and surely it should adapt to the new environment? While these debates raged, NATO found itself being used as the military wing of the United Nations in the former Yugoslavia, because the UN did not possess a standing military force. The relationship between NATO commanders and UN commanders is often portrayed as somewhat strained, due to the different aims of the two organisations. The Supreme Allied Commander, Europe during much of the crisis was General George Joulwan, who it is widely reported had intense rows with his UN counterpart, General Sir Michael Rose. Slightly down the chain of command, the responsibility for carrying out the air strikes resided with the Commander in Chief Allied Forces South (CINCSOUTH), Admiral Leighton Smith. Admiral Smith was another American, based in Italy, and was keen to neutralise Serb air defences before initiating a massive air strike in order to reduce the risk to his multinational pilots. The key differences concerning the two organisations with regard to strategy revolved around the fact that only the UN had large-scale forces on the ground, whereas NATO (at the time) held very much a supporting role in the form of air assets. Therefore, if NATO adopted a tough line and bombed Serb positions intensively, it would be the 'light' UN forces that would have to endure the inevitable Serb retaliation.

Europe

In Europe, nations were again quite divided over the best strategy to stop the fighting in Croatia and Bosnia-Herzegovina. The will of the European Community (EC) to engage in the diplomacy to halt the fighting was only as strong as the collective unity of its member-states. In Slovenia, the EC had significant success with the Treaty of Brioni, but after that high point European Union (EU) diplomacy (the EC was renamed the EU in 1993) struggled to apply effective pressure on the warring sides. Lord Carrington, the first official mediator, failed to get consensus within the divided European nations and resigned in 1992, to be replaced by another British politician, Lord Owen. The Vance-Owen Peace Plan of 1993 and the Owen-Stoltenberg Plan in August of the same year both failed, and by 1994 EU diplomacy had been overshadowed by the new Contact Group made up of Britain, France, Germany, Russia and the United States. The problem for the Europeans was the level of division between major nations as to the best way forward. Germany, under the leadership of Helmut Kohl and his Foreign Minister, Hans Dietrich Genscher, took the lead with the recognition of the Balkan states, but upset Britain and France in the process. Germany also accommodated the bulk of the refugees fleeing Bosnia-Herzegovina. However, Germany was preoccupied with major issues at home during this time, such as the costs of reunification with East Germany, and the task of trying to re-establish itself as a united country within the European continent, as well as international relations as a whole.

France under President François Mitterrand initially opposed recognition of the Balkan states, but proved to be a stalwart of the contributing nations to the peacekeeping effort in the region. Like the British, the French were also opposed to the plans to deploy thousands of extra soldiers to make the safe areas work.

A European Community Observer monitoring the fighting in Croatia in 1991 and gathering evidence. (Photo by Gilles BASSIGNAC/ Gamma-Rapho via Getty Images)

The United Kingdom

The British position under Prime Minister John Major, Foreign Secretary Douglas Hurd, and Defence Secretary Malcolm Rifkind is probably the most contentious because it was so firmly against decisive military involvement to end the fighting. Indeed, the term 'serbophile' is often used by critics to describe Britain's policy towards the Serbs.

The level to which the unhealthy relationship between influential British politicians and a Serbian politician subsequently arrested for crimes against humanity had

The UN general who ended the fighting. Lieutenant General Rupert Smith arrives in Sarajevo in January 1995. (ENRIC MARTI/AFP via Getty Images)

descended was revealed when Douglas Hurd (having retired from office and now working for industry) travelled to Belgrade in 1996 to try to obtain a contract with Milosevic's government to offer advice on privatisation. On the ground, British military commanders like General Sir Michael Rose struggled to find a balance between peacekeeping and active involvement in the fighting at a level that the British Government, the UN, and the people of the Balkans would all find satisfactory. The appointment of General Sir Rupert Smith, however, brought about a change not only in how affairs were run in the UN headquarters on the ground, but also in the interpretation of the UN mandate. British policy fundamentally changed in 1995, as a result of a military leader who had the moral courage to do what was needed to end the fighting decisively. Britain, perhaps above all nations in Europe, bears a great deal of responsibility for the tragedy that engulfed the former Yugoslavia, and yet at the same time played an important part in getting humanitarian aid to those that needed it. This seemingly absurd contradiction symbolised the disjointed European approach to the Balkan problem – it could end the fighting, but out of choice allowed the bloodshed to continue while distributing medical supplies to everyone.

Involvement of other nations

On the wings of the conflict, a number of nations, organisations and collective bodies became steadily involved. The new Russia under President Boris Yeltsin and his special envoy to the region, Vitaly Churkin, sent peacekeepers for UNPROFOR operations and developed a good relationship with their fellow Slavs, but it was a relationship that was often overstated by the West. It was easy to forget that Yugoslavia, despite all the Soviet-style weapons, was not part of the Warsaw Pact and actually feared Soviet intervention throughout the Cold War. Indeed, Russia often supported the use of NATO air strikes at various stages of the conflict. Islamic nations demonstrated their support for the plight of the Bosniaks through the Organisation of Islamic Countries, which Bosnia-Herzegovina joined, but much of this support was in the form of humanitarian supplies and medical teams, though Iran managed to smuggle weapons to the Bosniaks. The UN peacekeeping effort accepted soldiers, policemen, medics and observers from a wide range of continents. From Africa came assistance from Ghana, Kenya and Nigeria. The Americas despatched peacekeepers from Argentina, Brazil, Canada, Columbia, the United States and Venezuela. Asian nations as diverse as Bangladesh, Indonesia, Malaysia, Nepal and Pakistan also sent significant numbers of troops. European states such as Belgium, Britain, Finland, France, Ireland, Lithuania, the Netherlands, Norway, Poland, Portugal, Russia, Slovak Republic, Spain, Sweden, Switzerland, and on the fringe of the continent, Turkey and Ukraine, all sent peacekeepers. In the Middle East, countries like Egypt, Jordan and Tunisia contributed forces to the humanitarian effort, and on the other side of the world even New Zealand sent manpower.

Other organisations that tried hard to stop the fighting in the former Yugoslavia included the Conference on Security and Cooperation in Europe (CSCE), which was renamed the Organisation for Security and Cooperation in Europe (OSCE) in 1994. It tackled the growing refugee crisis in 1992, and unlike NATO, which was a very exclusive organisation limited to a select number of member states, the CSCE encompassed over 50 nations. At an early stage in the fighting, it was discussed whether the Western European Union (WEU), the European security organisation, could have a unilateral role, but this proposal was quickly dropped. The economic damage caused by the warfare meant that both the International Monetary Fund (IMF) and the World Bank would have to play a significant part in the reconstruction of the region. In Bosnia-Herzegovina, it was estimated that gross domestic product (GDP) had fallen by 70 per cent, and industry, agriculture and infrastructure, from roads to houses, were all badly damaged. It would take billions of dollars to get this country, let alone Croatia, back to normal. The sanctions regime on Serbia and Montenegro meant that their economies were also in bad shape, especially Serbia, due to Milosevic's disastrous economic policies. Non-Governmental Organisations (NGOs) played a very important part in bringing relief to the suffering people, from the International Committee of the Red Cross (ICRC) to the extremely brave medics of Medecins Sans Frontières (MSF), to name but a few of those that risked their lives on a daily basis.

The media

The role of the international media in bringing to the world's attention what many politicians in Europe were frantically trying to downplay cannot be underestimated in finally contributing to the end of the fighting. One of the most important media moments of the conflict was when the British reporter Penny Marshall, working for ITN, filmed the horrific conditions of inmates at the detention centre at Omarska in 1992. Overnight, the fighting in the Balkans brought home to

audiences around the world how quickly Europe had returned to the past – death camps and genocide existed once more. The images of people starved to the point that ribs began to be clearly visible, and drawn faces talking to the press from behind barbed wire, must be the defining images of the Balkan Wars. Other reporters, such as Roy Gutmann of Newsday, Misha Glenny of the BBC World Service, and Maggie O'Kane and Ed Vulliamy of *The Guardian*, stand out as some of the most influential voices about the conflict. The famous man in the white suit, Martin Bell of the BBC, was a popular figure on international television, and he was wounded while reporting from Sarajevo. CNN, as usual, was an immensely powerful instrument for shaping popular perceptions, and Richard Holbrooke became noted for his adept use of this media outlet. Overall, the Balkans was a dangerous place for

The Red Cross playing its vital role in helping and monitoring prisoner exchanges between all sides. (Photo by Antoine GYORI – Corbis/Sygma via Getty Images)

The horrific images of starving prisoners from Omarska in 1992 profoundly affected how the situation in the former Yugoslavia was perceived internationally. They resurrected the spectres of death camps and genocide in Europe again. (Photo by Antoine GYORI – Corbis/ Sygma via Getty Images)

journalists, with many being arrested as spies or simply cut down by snipers. Consequently, many journalists stuck with the UN forces in certain areas for protection purposes, and this naturally influenced their viewpoint. For example, media coverage in the British-operating areas in Central Bosnia was very good, but other areas received less attention. An aspect of the media side of the conflict that received very little attention was Milosevic's use of state-run media outlets to keep the bulk of the people in Serbia uninformed as to the true extent of the slaughter being committed in their name. Of course, indications of the barbarity would be evident from conscripts returning from the frontlines, but in many ways the media was a key weapon in Serbia's arsenal. Unsurprisingly, NATO's plans in the subsequent war over Kosovo in 1999 contained a significant media strategy, to combat the enormous levels of propaganda that Milosevic's regime was capable of churning out to keep the Serbian people loyal to his cause.

HOW THE WAR ENDED

From peacekeeping to peace enforcement

By July 1995, the efforts of the United Nations to bring peace to Yugoslavia looked doomed to failure, and its international credibility was rapidly diminishing. The UN would make firm declarations to the international community, and when challenged by the Bosnian Serbs would fall back and accede to their demands. While the UN's position became increasingly undermined with each atrocity and humiliation on the ground, the effect on the Bosnian Serbs was quite the opposite. The fall of Srebrenica greatly encouraged them to continue their aggression against the safe areas, and a few weeks later on 25 July 1995, Mladic's men managed to seize another safe area – Zepa. Once more, the international community appeared paralysed by events on the ground in Bosnia-Herzegovina, and even the UN Human Rights Advocate, Tadeusz Mazowiecki, resigned in protest over the flagrant breaches of human rights. However, specific operational measures were under discussion that would radically transform the situation. As Zepa fell to the advancing Bosnian Serbs, the North Atlantic Council (the decision-making body within NATO) agreed on a new policy of air strikes as part of a sustained campaign, rather than close air support operations, to protect the remaining safe areas of Bihac, Tuzla and Sarajevo. In concert with the

United Nations, the command and control system to initiate such a response was also changed, giving the 'key' to the Force Commander in theatre, or in his absence to the UNPROFOR commander in Bosnia-Herzegovina. In simple terms, if the key was 'turned' then action would occur immediately – not just one or two bombs, but a sustained offensive.

Operation *Storm*

Events on the ground were also about to change for different strategic reasons. The official and unofficial aid (civilian and military) that the United States had given to the Croatian Army was now about to bear fruit. On 4 August, the revitalised and US-trained Croatian forces initiated Operation *Storm*, or *Oluja*, which was designed to decisively capture the Croatian Serb area of the Krajina. The Croats had built up an army of 200,000 soldiers for this operation, and attacked in a pincer movement with a heavy emphasis on the capture of the strategically important capital, Knin. Following a lightning heavy bombardment of Serb positions, the Croatian forces

Victorious Croatian soldiers celebrating their part in the stunning success of Operation *Storm* in 1995 that witnessed the capture of Republika Srpska Krajina in just three days. (ILIE BUMBAC/AFP via Getty Images)

moved forward with remarkable ease. The Croatian Serb forces had about 40,000 troops and 400 tanks to defend the region, but these were caught out by the speed and direction of the offensive. In just three days, Republika Srpska Krajina (RSK) was largely overrun by the victorious Croatian Army, and the capital of Knin captured; almost 200,000 Serbs fled into Bosnia-Herzegovina. Despite assurances from President Tudjman that civilians would not be harmed, there were widespread indications of atrocities against the Serbs who stayed behind, and entire villages were razed to the ground.

This tremendous military victory rapidly altered the strategic and diplomatic context in the Balkans, and the Croatian forces and their Bosniak allies in Bihac began to make significant inroads into the Serb-controlled regions.

The Markale Market massacre, part II

The trigger for the use of decisive force against the Bosnian Serbs by NATO forces was the firing of five mortar shells at the busy Markale Market on the morning of 28 August 1995. Thirty-seven people were killed and around 90 wounded in the attack. Interestingly, a year earlier, an identical attack in which 68 people were killed had prompted the then UNPROFOR commander, General Rose, to blame Bosniaks as a result of a flawed forensic report. This time, the report into the shelling clearly identified that the shells had originated from the Bosnian Serb positions around Lukavica. Unlike his predecessor, General Sir Rupert Smith did not solely pursue the negotiations option in the aftermath of the massacre with a view to seeking another fragile agreement. Instead, the British commander exploited the situation to bring about a resolution once and for all. By fortunate coincidence, the UN Force Commander in Zagreb was out of theatre, and so the 'key' to initiate air strikes resided in the hands of General Smith.

Commemorating the Markale Market massacre in 2019. In 1994, a Bosnian Serb mortar shell killed 68 people in a crowded market. It happened again in 1995 and provoked NATO intervention. (Photo by Samir Yordamovic/Anadolu Agency/Getty Images)

One constraint on the immediate recourse to air strikes was the presence of UN forces passing through Bosnian Serb territory near Gorazde. It is important to note that Serb tactics of taking hostages after a close air support strike had not been lost on UNPROFOR, and consequently in the weeks leading up to late August 1995 NATO had deliberately withdrawn its forces from exposed positions. Having received the report into the attack on Sarajevo, General Smith employed a clever dual-track psychological approach to ensure the safe passage of his troops through the Bosnian Serb lines. First, during a phone call with General Mladic, the UNPROFOR commander neglected to mention that he now knew who had fired the mortars and that he was planning direct military action. Consequently, Mladic was lulled into a false sense of security, and let the UN forces pass out of the territory unhindered. Secondly, General Smith released a statement to the press that was very vague on the subjects of either who was to blame for the attack that morning, or what the response of the international community would be. To any seasoned observer of Balkan affairs on the night of 28 August, it looked like the UN would once more revert to inactivity, and acquiesce to yet another atrocity.

Operation *Deliberate Force*

At 2000hrs on 28 August 1995, General Sir Rupert Smith turned his key. He did so without consulting the UN (who found out about this decision six hours later) or the nations who were contributing troops to UNPROFOR, and talked instead with the head of NATO's Southern Command, who would initiate the air strikes. Both men were in agreement that the air strikes would commence as soon as NATO forces were ready and the weather improved. At 0300hrs on 30 August, Operation *Deliberate Force* began in earnest, with the aim of significantly degrading the ability of the Bosnian Serb forces entrenched around Sarajevo to harm either the civilians or UNPROFOR forces. The Rapid Reaction Force was an essential component of the strategy to neutralise Bosnian Serb artillery positions, and came equipped with heavy artillery. On the first night of operations they fired 600 rounds of heavy calibre, high explosive ordnance on Bosnian Serb artillery positions around Sarajevo. UNPROFOR guns located on Mount Igman bracketed 19 Bosnian Serb positions with devastatingly accurate shell-fire in order to coerce them

US naval air power in the form of F-18 Hornets and an F-14 Tomcat ready for operations in the Adriatic Sea from the strike carrier USS *Theodore Roosevelt*. (VINCENT AMALVY/AFP via Getty Images)

into withdrawing out of the 20km exclusion zone around Sarajevo. The terms under which Operation *Deliberate Force* would be halted were unambiguous – the Bosnian Serbs must respect the safe zones around the remaining safe areas, and stop fighting not only in these areas, but across the entire country. The cost to the NATO forces on the first night of operations was extremely light, with one French Mirage aircraft shot down and some ineffective small arms fire being directed at UNPROFOR positions.

Negotiations continued throughout the bombing, and a lull in the air strikes on 31 August caused by bad weather allowed the Force Commander, General Janvier (who had returned to the region), to implement a strategic pause in operations on 1 September in order to initiate talks with General Mladic at Zvornik. In addition, General Smith used this period to open up the road between Sarajevo and its airport on 2 September, and warned the Bosnian Serbs that if they prevented the free flow of traffic, the consequences would be extremely severe. A day later he also opened up a land route from the city to Butmir. In effect, General Smith had broken the siege of Sarajevo and people could move freely on these routes, without fear of roadblock or shootings, for the first time in three years. The talks with Mladic and the Bosnian Serb leadership predictably failed, and air strikes continued on 5 September. To the consternation of the UN hierarchy, UNPROFOR started issuing statements that they would 'cripple' the military capabilities of the Bosnian Serbs. In concert with these threats, NATO aircraft started to hit targets outside of Sarajevo (labelled 'Option 3') from 6 September onwards, mainly because they had run out of the so-called Option 2 targets around the city. These Option targets were Serbian positions of military and economic value, from anti-aircraft missile sites to communications centres that included television and radio transmitters. These could be targeted with an array of weapons, from precision-guided munitions to 'dumb' bombs. Again, negotiations between the three sides continued throughout the bombing, and the United States diplomat Richard Holbrooke interfaced with the highest levels of the three political structures. On 10 September, NATO increased the pressure on the Bosnian Serbs by firing 13 Tomahawk missiles at the air defence sites around Banja Luka. Bit by bit, General Mladic's forces were being taken apart by NATO forces, finally dispelling the prevalent myth that hundreds of thousands of troops would be required to bring the Bosnian Serbs under control. By 14 September the negotiations had made surprising progress, and once more a pause was put into effect regarding the air strikes. The Bosnian Serbs completely complied with all the terms set out by the UN, and Operation *Deliberate Force* was formally ended on 21 September.

NATO aircraft flew over 3,000 sorties in support of Operation *Deliberate Force*, and attacked more than 60 targets on the ground. In concert with UNPROFOR artillery units, these attacks demonstrated that the Bosnian Serb forces were little more than a paper tiger. The military situation for

An UNPROFOR air base in Tuzla. (Photo by David Brauchli/ Sygma via Getty Images)

the Bosnian Serbs went from bad to worse throughout this offensive, as Croatian and Bosniak forces captured more territory. The proportion of Bosnia-Herzegovina controlled by the Bosnian Serbs fell rapidly by around 20 per cent. It became increasingly clear that the Bosnian Serb military leadership was out of its league. General Mladic's military reputation was quickly exposed by General Sir Rupert Smith as one built on bluff and fighting much weaker forces. General Smith was a man with vastly more military experience, who had led an armoured division in the Gulf War of 1991. It was a moral and military victory for a soldier who avoided the limelight, and never forgot his humanity. Operation *Deliberate Force* remains a little-known example of how a seemingly intractable conflict can be resolved though the robust interpretation of a UN peacekeeping mandate.

CONCLUSION AND CONSEQUENCES
The Dayton Agreement

Against the background of the intense NATO bombing and UN shelling of Bosnian Serb positions, the United States took the diplomatic lead to finally conclude the fighting in the Balkans. Negotiations since the Vance-Owen Peace Plan had never really succeeded in generating a plan to which all sides would be happy to subscribe. Several proposals were put forward in the years 1993 to 1995, one envisaging three republics in Bosnia-Herzegovina, and another pressing for a 51:49 split of territory between the Bosniaks and Croats, and the Bosnian Serbs. By 1995, however, the Americans realised that all of these plans, whether by the EU, the Contact Group or the United Nations, would not succeed unless they took charge of the negotiating process. This is the most interesting facet of the Dayton Agreement held at the Wright-Patterson Air Force base in Dayton, Ohio. A recent memoir by General Wesley Clark, who played a very important part in the process, reveals that the US chief negotiator, Richard Holbrooke, was well aware that the Serbs and Bosniaks were quite capable of creating divisions amongst the Europeans, or turning them against the Americans. Relegating the Europeans to a supporting role in essence prevented such a scenario from developing. In addition, military events on the ground had

RIGHT America's negotiator, Richard Holbrooke, commemorates the fifth anniversary of the Dayton Peace Accords in 2000. (DAVID MAXWELL/AFP via Getty Images)

THE DAYTON AGREEMENT, 21 NOVEMBER 1995

CROATIA

Prijedor

Bihac

REPUBLIC SRPSKA

Banja Luka

Tuzla

Zenica

BOSNIA AND
HERZEGOVINA

Srebrenica

Sarajevo   Pale

Gorazde

Adriatic Sea   Mostar

N

—— Dayton Agreement Line

0   50 miles

0   100 km

FEDERAL REPUBLIC OF YUGOSLAVIA

ABOVE The Dayton Agreement effectively ended the fighting in the former Yugoslavia with the introduction of the Implementation Force (IFOR) into the region, and the creation of the Office of the High Representative (OHR) to direct civil affairs.

greatly helped the US negotiations, as the Croatian and Bosniak offensives had just about created the desired 51:49 division of territory that was long perceived as a workable framework for the future.

The negotiating positions of the three major regional powers at Dayton offer an insight into individual perspectives by 1995. The Serbian negotiating stance was fascinating, in the sense that Milosevic dominated the agenda and refused to allow the Bosnian Serbs to torpedo the talks. Perhaps for a brief moment in time a veil had been lifted, and the true balance of power as well as the hierarchy of command was finally revealed at Dayton. For Milosevic, time was beginning to run out. The wars had been disastrous for the Serbian economy, sanctions had hit his regime hard, and the international reputation of Serbs had been sullied. Milosevic's casual abandonment of the Croatian Serbs and then the Bosnian Serbs demonstrated that they had been merely puppets for his own political ambitions, and when they had served their purposes he dropped them with alacrity. Of course, he tried to fashion the agreement to suit his purposes, and attempted to delay the arrival of foreign troops or limit their powers, but the United States refused to be drawn into yet another Balkan trick. At the end of the day, Milosevic was a political survivor. His attempts to play the nationalist card in both Croatia and Bosnia-Herzegovina had backfired badly, and it was now time to shore up his own regime in Serbia itself. The Croatian position under Tudjman was a reluctantly practical one. After all, it was American assistance that had formed the platform for Croatian military successes in 1995, and the withdrawal of that support would have very significant consequences. Tudjman strongly supported the Bosnian Croats, who were dissatisfied with the dominance of the Bosniaks in parts of the Federation, and aspired to an autonomous area like the Serbs, but the will of the international community was strong enough to keep these nationalistic tendencies under control. The biggest winners in the entire process were the Bosniaks, who managed to involve the world's only remaining superpower in their region in a political, economic and military sense. Izetbegovic tried hard to expand US involvement in as much of the Bosniak-Croat Federation as possible, on all levels – from policing to military operations. His strategy was quite simple: the ineffectiveness of the Europeans in resolving the crisis meant that the best hope for peace and security for Bosniaks lay with the United States. In this respect, Dayton was a triumph for the victims of Serbian aggression.

Operation *Joint Endeavour* and Operation *Joint Guard*

The Dayton process culminated in a document called 'The General Framework Agreement', which was initialled by all three parties on 21 November before being formally signed at a ceremony in Paris on 14 December 1995. The paper set out in eleven annexes how the peace would be maintained, and included military aspects as well as regional stabilisation, inter-entity boundaries, elections, the constitution, arbitration, human rights, refugees and displaced persons, national monuments, public corporations and an international police task force. A new civil administration called the Office of the High Representative (OHR), the first of which was the Swedish politician Carl Bildt, was created to run the country. To make this comprehensive accord work, a large military formation called the Implementation Force (IFOR), comprising 60,000 soldiers, was deployed to Bosnia and Herzegovina in a plan called Operation *Joint Endeavour*. Unlike UNPROFOR, whose mandate ended with the deployment of IFOR, this was a NATO unit of which a third of the troops were from the United States and who possessed all the accoutrements for war, from tanks to supporting artillery. Remarkably, IFOR began deploying in Bosnia and Herzegovina just six days after the signing of the accord in Paris.

IFOR's mandate was to last exactly one year, when it would be replaced by a new formation called the Stabilisation Force, or SFOR (Operation *Joint Guard*), which would be half its size. Unlike UNPROFOR, IFOR could 'compel' any of the parties that were interfering with its mandate on the ground, or in other words, engage in robust peace enforcement.

NEXT PAGES
Signing the peace. Milosevic, Tudjman and Izetbegovic sit uncomfortably together after signing the peace accords under the gaze of international leaders. (Photo by Peter Turnley/ Corbis/VCG via Getty Images)

PAIX SUR L'EX-YOUGOSLAVIE
PARIS

As such it was extremely successful, and finally a sense of normality began to return to Bosnia and Herzegovina. IFOR's successor, SFOR, was reduced considerably from its peak size of 32,000 to around 7,000 before the mission was handed over the EU in December 2004, with some NATO support available to this new organisation under the rubric of *EUFOR Operation ALTHEA*. SFOR achieved much in its time, from active patrols to arresting war criminals (21 by 2000), and helping to rebuild the shattered infrastructure of the country. Under the auspices of Operation *Harvest*, SFOR troops have collected around 11,000 weapons and over 40,000 hand grenades, as well as destroying over 2 million unsafe munitions from bombs to land mines. These forces have been instrumental in opening up safe routes for the civilians of Bosnia and Herzegovina and ensuring a level of security for people on all sides that was continued by *EUFOR Operation ALTHEA*.

The War in Kosovo, 1999

It is perhaps ironic that the very place where Milosevic had built up his political powerbase and reputation would ultimately prove to be his Achilles heel. The issue of autonomy had always been at the heart of the dispute between the majority Kosovan Albanians and the minority Serbs, who represented around 10 per cent of the population. These tensions that had been quite apparent at the end of the 1980s began to manifest themselves from 1996 onwards in terms of violence. By 1998, Serb forces (Army and Special Police Units) were openly fighting what they described as a terrorist organisation, the Kosovo Liberation Army (UCK), and launched a major offensive that was characterised by killings, burning villages and forcing over 200,000 Kosovans to flee in fear. For the watching international community, it was all too familiar, as Milosevic applied his usual strategy for dealing with opposition. The consequences of a hands-off approach had already been demonstrated in the Balkan Wars of the early 1990s, and inevitably the regional costs would include the economic burden of feeding hundreds of thousands of refugees, as well as the real danger of spill-over in areas like Macedonia. The negotiating process revolved around the Contact Group, Richard Holbrooke, the United Nations, the Organisation for Security and Cooperation in Europe (OSCE) and NATO, with the latter organisation taking a noticeable lead in terms of willingness to apply force to resolve the issue. In September 1998, the UN Security Council passed UNSCR 1199, which pushed for a ceasefire and the pull-back of military forces in Kosovo. In support of this diplomacy, NATO initiated activation orders for air strikes, and Holbrooke held face-to-face talks with Milosevic, eventually persuading him to accept two verification missions, one by NATO from the air called Operation *Eagle Eye*, and the other by the OSCE on the ground called the Kosovo Verification Mission. This agreement was rubber-stamped by the UN with the passing of UNSCR 1203. These verification missions that started in November revealed that Serb forces continued to flout the will of the international community, and in January 1999 found apparently hard evidence of a massacre of 45 Kosovo Albanians at a village called Racak. This incident helped to push all sides towards getting a meaningful resolution of the dispute, and talks were initiated between Milosevic, the leader of the shadow government of the Kosovo Albanians, Dr Ibrahim Rugova, and the Contact Group, at Rambouillet in France on 6 February 1999. The first round of talks failed to reached a comprehensive settlement, and a second round, or the 'Paris Follow-On Talks' (15–18 March), led to the Kosovo Albanians signing up to an agreement that would allow a NATO-organised force into Kosovo itself. Milosevic, however, refused to accept such a proposition. In typical fashion, he had launched a major offensive in Kosovo while

ABOVE The fighting starts again in Kosovo between the Kosovo Liberation Army fighters and Serb forces in 1999. (Photo By David Brauchli/Getty Images)

RIGHT Relatives and friends grieve for the victims of the Racak massacre in Kosovo who were buried in February 1999. (Photo by Chris Hondros/Getty Images) the talks were taking place, and was using the negotiations to merely build up his units so that he could dictate his own terms on the ground. On 22 March, last-minute face-to-face talks between Richard Holbrooke and Milosevic in Belgrade failed, prompting NATO's Secretary General, Javier Solana, in consultation with the alliance members, to order SACEUER (Supreme Allied Commander, Europe) General Wesley Clark to start the campaign the next day. NATO's air operations began on 24 March 1999.

Operation *Allied Force*

In retrospect, Operation *Allied Force* was a somewhat unusual and disjointed campaign for a military organisation that was celebrating its fiftieth anniversary. In the run-up to conflict, NATO had planned for a wide range of contingencies concerning the use of force over Kosovo, but the failure of the negotiations appeared to catch the alliance by surprise. In a military sense, it certainly did not have enough aircraft in the theatre at the start of hostilities (these would grow steadily in number throughout the 78 days of bombing), and politically, divisions began to emerge amongst NATO countries when the bombing started. Consequently, these factors meant that the performance of the initial strategy and the effectiveness of NATO strikes were very mixed. In addition to the shortage of strike aircraft (just 120 on 24 March, rising to over 300 by the end of April), which reduced NATO's ability to initiate a *Desert Storm* style of air offensive, the awful weather over the region severely degraded NATO ability to hit targets effectively. Consequently, the first phases of the campaign were indecisive and had a frustratingly slow effect on Serbian ethnic cleansing on the ground in Kosovo, which accelerated enormously with 800,000 of Kosovo's population having been expelled by May. The campaign only started to have an impact when NATO escalated its bombing strategy to

include Serbia itself, and neutralised power stations with graphite (soft bombs), and destroyed 34 bridges, 57 per cent of Serbia's oil reserves, and all of the Yugoslav oil refineries. It was this ability to bring the war to the Serbian people, especially after the destruction of Serb radio and television in Belgrade on 23 April, that placed enormous pressure on Milosevic's regime. The United States bore the burden of the campaign, contributing the bulk of the attack aircraft, which included B-52s, B-1B bombers and B-2 Stealth Bombers, which flew 30-hour missions from their base in Missouri! Over 300 cruise missiles were fired during the course of the 78-day action. However, it was a very limited campaign in comparison with previous wars, with just 37,000 air sorties dropping an estimated 23,000 munitions, of which 35 per cent were precision-guided weapons, about four times the amount used during the Gulf War of 1991. In addition, despite not suffering a single fatality in combat, an F-16 and an F-117 Stealth Fighter were shot down. Tragically, the Chinese Embassy was also bombed on 7 May by accident, by a B-2 bomber with satellite-guided bombs (Joint Direct Attack Munitions – JDAMs), and the cause of this error was put down to using out-of-date maps. By early June it was quite clear that Milosevic was ready to negotiate, and on 9 June a military-technical agreement was signed between NATO and the Yugoslav authorities, which encompassed the withdrawal of Serb forces from Kosovo. UNSCR 1244 was passed the next day, which allowed a multinational force under Lieutenant General Sir Michael Jackson (UK) to enter Kosovo to ensure peace and security, where they discovered evidence of widespread abuses of human rights.

OPPOSITE US F-16s based in Italy conduct operations in support of Operation *Allied Force* in 1999. (GREG L. DAVIS/ AFP via Getty Images)

The fall of Milosevic

The new millennium was a bad year for Milosevic and his former associates and rivals. In January 2000, the notorious

Arkan was shot dead outside a fashionable Belgrade hotel, and great mystery surrounds who was behind his killing. Arkan naturally had many enemies, but he was also a major figure in Serbia's criminal elite that controlled vast portions of the economy. Suspicions have fallen on Milosevic's son, Marko, who was also allegedly heavily involved in this underworld, or Milosevic himself, who may have feared that Arkan might 'spill the beans' to the International Criminal Tribunal for the former Yugoslavia (ICTY). Or perhaps it was just gangster rivals. In August 2000, a former ally of Milosevic, Ivan Stambolic, suddenly disappeared without trace. Milosevic stood for re-election as Yugoslav President in autumn 2000, and despite losing substantially to his main rival, Vojislav Kostunica, the leader of the Democratic Party of Serbia, 'Slobo' tried to rig the elections as he had done on several occasions in the past. Nearly half a million people rose up in protest over this tactic on 5 October in Belgrade, and stormed the Parliament before setting fire to it. It was the last straw for the Serbian people, and Kostunica was propelled into power while Milosevic, realising that the game was up, retired to his Belgrade mansion. Under a dynamic Prime Minister, Zoran Djindjic, who was well aware of the need to improve relations with the international community, Milosevic was arrested in April 2001, before being handed over to the international court at The Hague in late June.

Milosevic's trial started in February 2002, and proved unsurprisingly to be a difficult legal case to prosecute. Unlike everyone else who died in brutal circumstances in the former Yugoslavia, Milosevic enjoyed all the privileges of civil rights, legal advice and protection while being examined. This was the first time a former head of state was put on trial – an important global precedent – and involved Serbian state secrets and a leader whose criminal tendencies were well documented. Nevertheless, notwithstanding all the challenges, the trial uncovered evidence of how important Serbia's role was in sustaining the fighting in Bosnia and Herzegovina and also in Croatia in terms of financial and military support for the Serb forces in these countries. Without Milosevic and Serbia, it is highly likely the fighting would have ended much earlier. It also brought to light harrowing footage of a Serbian force called the Scorpions linked to the Serbian police murdering people from Srebrenica. This actually had a profound impact in Serbia because Milosevic had carefully controlled the media during his time in power. Serbian citizens were quite unaware of the atrocities being carried out in the name of the Serb state. Unfortunately, a few months before the trial was due to conclude, Milosevic died of a heart attack. Would he have been convicted? This is one of the most contested aspects of the unfortunate ending of the case because, as with all things associated with the legal discipline, it is open to interpretation. What can be said is that Milosevic, despite his best efforts, faced justice for a time period measured in years! The wealth of information revealed by the trial has greatly altered historical understanding concerning the role of Serbia in sustaining the instability in the former Yugoslavia. Serbia, in this critical time, was without question under the direct political control and direction of President Milosevic.

The enterprising and brave Zoran Djindjic was assassinated in March 2003 by a former special police unit called the 'Red Berets', and during the course of the investigation the body of former President Ivan Stambolic was found. Interestingly, Milosevic's wife, Mirjana Markovic, and their son Marko have been implicated in Stambolic's murder as well as organised criminal activities, as once more the Red Berets (under direct orders) appeared to have committed this assassination. Both mother and son fled to Russia to escape an arrest warrant by Serbian police for their involvement in various crimes. The so-called 'Lady Macbeth' of the Balkans, Mirjana Markovic, died in Russia in 2019. Marko remains at large, probably still in Russia, which granted him and his mother 'refugee

A Serbian revolution. Citizens of Belgrade celebrate the departure of Slobodan Milosevic from power. (Photo by Braca Nadezdic/ Newsmakers/ Stringer/Getty Images)

status'. On top of these startling revelations, Serbia's former President, Milan Milutinovic (another ally of Milosevic), handed himself in to The Hague in January 2003 on charges of being a suspected war criminal, but was cleared in 2009.

The future

It is interesting to note that most of the major regional and international politicians involved in the Balkan Wars have bowed out of the public gaze in one form or another. Franjo Tudjman died in 1999, and Alija Izetbegovic passed away in 2003. Slobodan Milosevic died while on trial at The Hague while still being prosecuted for war crimes in Croatia, Bosnia and Herzegovina, and Kosovo. John Major and Douglas Hurd, to name two of the British officials, have become elder statesmen though it must have been uncomfortable watching the prosecution of a leader for war crimes whom they had treated with undue respect. President Bill Clinton retired from office, though probably with the most honours for his efforts in resolving the fighting. Prime Minister Tony Blair, who was firmly behind the military action in Kosovo and deserves great credit for his actions, found himself mired in controversy over allegations of unwarranted aggression with American allies in the Iraq War of 2003. The great negotiator Richard Holbrooke retired from public office for a time and resumed public life once more for the Obama administration as special representative to Afghanistan and Pakistan. Sadly, he died while undergoing surgery in 2010. General Wesley Clark retired not only from the US Army in 2000, but also from the race to become the Democratic Party's nominee for President in 2004. At The Hague, the ICTY fulfilled its mandate between 1993 and 2017 with the indictment of 161 key figures on all sides involved in the war crimes in the former Yugoslavia. Some are serving life sentences behind bars, some were acquitted and others have

Former Serbian President Milan Milutinovic heads toward his trial at The Hague in 2003. He was acquitted of all charges in 2009. (MICHAEL KOOREN/AFP via Getty Images)

served their sentences. One the most senior figures who has served her time was Biljana Plavsic (former Vice-President to Radovan Karadzic), sentenced to 11 years in jail for her activities. Radovan Karadzic was found (as the first edition of this book suggested) in Belgrade. He was pretending to be a new age healer with a bushy white beard when discovered by Serbian police who arrested him in 2008. Karadzic was found guilty on charges of genocide and war crimes in 2016 with a prison sentence of 40 years. An Appeal Court increased the sentence to life in prison in 2019. General Mladic was captured in 2011 after 14 years on the run in Serbia. Mladic

threatened people who sheltered him (often with suggestions about the wellbeing of their children) and became very reliant on family networks in his final years of 'freedom'. By the end, Mladic was sick, isolated and a shadow of the so-called 'Butcher of Bosnia' who rained terror and murder on the often-unarmed people and children of Bosnia and Herzegovina. Unsurprisingly, Mladic offered no resistance to the policeman who arrested him. Mladic was sentenced to life imprisonment in 2017 for war crimes, genocide and crimes against humanity. His appeal against his sentence was rejected in 2021.

The physical fighting is over, but the struggle to win the battle of narratives concerning blame and responsibility continues. One of the remarkable facets of the literature surrounding the collapse of Yugoslavia is the number of authors with close links to the region. That was very noticeable during the actual fighting in the early 1990s and continues to the present day. It poses a challenge to readers who are new to the area and requires a holistic approach to grasp the messaging beneath the various competing narratives. The former Yugoslavia has also sparked a vibrant research industry since the end of the fighting in 1999 that spans doctoral research, fieldwork, interviews, data collection and ethnographic studies. It has provoked substantial work in the areas of humanitarian intervention, sexual violence and rape in war, feminist perspectives, and knowledge production, to list just some of them. Nevertheless, the Balkans as subject does raise concerns with regard to the memorialisation of the conflict and the impact of paid research and interviews on collective understandings of what actually happened. There is still a very large diaspora of refugees from the former Yugoslavia who remain outside the region and whose children are now established citizens of other European states. This represents a significant cultural and social loss of an entire generation of Yugoslavs who could be contributing to

PREVIOUS PAGES
Spectators watching a giant screen at the Srebrenica-Potocari Memorial and Cemetery in 2021 celebrate the rejection of Ratko Mladic's appeal against his 2017 life sentence for war crimes, genocide and crimes against humanity. (Photo by Elman Omic/ Anadolu Agency via Getty Images)

rebuilding their societies. This is something that will take a very long time to overcome and impedes the rapid recovery of the devastated countries. Finally, it is also important to understand that the Dayton Agreement was never intended to be a long-term fix, so the onus is on the states of the former Yugoslavia to work with each other, and with regional and international partners, to find a permanent way forward. This is not easy in communities that still celebrate the memory of convicted war criminals as heroes in 2021. The hero-worship of convicted war criminals is perhaps the hardest facet for outsiders to understand. It raises an uncomfortable truth: genocide and ethnic cleansing require mass participation. The ICTY indicted just 161 individuals, but thousands were actively involved in the fighting. To systematically murder 8,000 people at Srebrenica took a massive effort, from those doing the killing to those providing the logistical support. It was a combination of state agencies, paramilitaries and private companies that made the genocide happen. For a community to accept that their leaders are criminals requires an uncomfortable gaze into the mirror. It also shows that the reconciliation of past injustices with present-day and future opportunities is, and will be, a long-term process in parts of the former Yugoslavia.

Why does the collapse of Yugoslavia matter today? It is a myth, albeit it a stubbornly persistent one, to think that what happened in the former Yugoslavia was in some way unique. It can happen anywhere. The awful events in the Balkans can be directly attributed to crass political irresponsibility. Put simply, the use of demagoguery wrapped in the flag of nationalism with a fair sprinkling of criminality. Milosevic was the epitome of this style of politics and used all the traditional means of propaganda, especially control of the media, to generate support and hatred for those he designated as the enemy. His Bosnian Serb proxies, in the former of Karadzic and Mladic, encouraged by Milosevic's rhetoric and outright

NEXT PAGES The full horror of life in besieged Sarajevo is testified by the overflow of graves into alternative areas including the famous Olympic Stadium because the cemeteries were full. (Photo by Patrick ROBERT – Corbis/ Sygma via Getty Images)

support, brought genocide back to the European continent. Sadly, other world leaders have adopted this approach and, surprisingly, they are not all located in the East. In January 2021, the world watched with horror as an out-of-control mob stormed the US Capitol and witnessed American politicians fleeing for their lives while brave policemen tried to hold back the protestors. A combination of social media and irresponsible comments from an embittered outgoing President created the conditions for a horrifying and very dangerous event to occur in the nation considered to be the leader of democracy in the free world. In the twenty-first century, the development of social media technologies has taken the ability to generate a mass information effect (what would be considered propaganda in times-gone-by) on a society or even an external nation state to another level of capability. It means that politicians have the tools to create the conditions for a Balkans-style catastrophe in a compressed timeframe. The horrible events of the collapse of Yugoslavia remain a *caveat emptor* ('let the buyer beware') for societies that permit the incendiary mixture of demagoguery, nationalism and criminality to become the acceptable face of politics. That is the key lesson of the tragedy that engulfed one of the most peaceful, vibrant and cosmopolitan regions of the world in a horrifyingly short time while the international community fumbled its response with devastating consequences.

CHRONOLOGY

1389	Battle of Kosovo Polje. Much of the Yugoslav region falls under the influence of the Ottoman Empire.
1878	Congress of Berlin. Serbia gains independence.
1908	Austria-Hungary annexes Bosnia and Herzegovina.
1914	**June** Archduke Franz Ferdinand is assassinated in Sarajevo. **August** Outbreak of World War I.
1919	Treaty of Versailles confirms the newly created Kingdom of Serbs, Croats and Slovenes, which also encompasses Bosnia-Herzegovina.
1929	The Kingdom of Serbs, Croats and Slovenes is renamed Yugoslavia.
1934	King Alexander of Yugoslavia is assassinated.
1939	Outbreak of World War II.
1941	**April** Germany invades Yugoslavia.
1945	Tito and the communists gain power.
1948	Tito falls out with Stalin.
1974	Tito's new constitution introduced.
1980	Tito dies.
1986	The controversial Memorandum from the Serbian Academy of Sciences is issued.
1987	Milosevic becomes leader of the Serbian League of Communists.
1989	Fall of the Berlin Wall.
1990	**January** League of Yugoslav Communists meets. **April** Elections in the republics.
1991	**25 June** Slovenia and Croatia declare their independence. **27 June** JNA deploys into Slovenia. Fighting breaks out. **7 July** Brioni Agreement. **July** Fighting breaks out in Croatia. **25 Sept** UN arms embargo comes into force.
1992	**January** UNPROFOR created. EC recognises Slovenia and Croatia. **1 March** Bosnian referendum on independence. Fighting breaks out later that month. **April** USA recognises Croatia, Slovenia and Bosnia-Herzegovina.

Serbia and Montenegro join forces to become the Federal Republic of Yugoslavia

August Journalists visit Omarska detention camp.

October The no-fly zone is set up.

1993   **January** The Vance-Owen Peace Plan is unveiled.

May The International Criminal Tribunal for the former Yugoslavia (ICTY) at The Hague is created.

April Large-scale fighting breaks out between the Bosniaks and Bosnian Croats.

1994   **February** The Markale Market in Sarajevo is mortared.

March NATO warplanes conduct air strikes. Owen-Stoltenberg Plan put forward. Bosniak-Bosnian Croat federation created.

April Gorazde attacked. British Sea Harrier shot down.

June Contact Group takes the diplomatic lead.

December Cessation of Hostilities Agreement (COHA).

1995   **June** Scott O'Grady is shot down.

July Srebrenica and Zepa fall. 8,000 Muslim men and boys massacred.

August Operation *Storm* captures the Krajina. The Markale Market is attacked by Bosnian Serb mortars. Operation *Deliberate Force* begins.

November Dayton Agreement.

December Peace signed in Paris. Implementation Force (IFOR) deploys into Bosnia and Herzegovina.

1998   Open fighting between Serbian forces and Kosovo Liberation Army.

September United Nations Security Council Resolution (UNSCR) 1199.

1999   **January** Racak massacre.

February Talks at Rambouillet.

March Failure of the Paris Follow-On Talks. Operation *Allied Force* begins.

April Serb Television and Radio in Belgrade attacked by NATO.

May Chinese Embassy in Belgrade hit by NATO bombs.

June Military-technical agreement signed. UNSCR 1244 passed.

2000   **January** Arkan shot dead in Belgrade.

August Ivan Stambolic disappears.

October Popular uprising against Milosevic. Milosevic retires from office. Vojislav Kostunica becomes Yugoslav President.

2001 **April** Serbian Prime Minister Zoran Djindjic allows Milosevic to be arrested.

June Milosevic is handed over to the ICTY at The Hague.

2002 **February** The trial of Milosevic for war crimes begins.

2003 **January** Serbian President Milan Milutinovic hands himself in to The Hague to face charges of being a suspected war criminal.

March Zoran Djindjic is assassinated.

2006 **March** Milosevic dies in prison during his trial.

2008 **July** Radovan Karadzic arrested.

2011 **May** General Mladic arrested.

2016 **March** Karadzic convicted for war crimes and genocide (40-year sentence).

2017 **November** Mladic convicted for crimes, genocide and crimes against humanity (life sentence).

2019 **March** Karadzic appeal dismissed. Sentence increased to life imprisonment.

2019 **April** Mirjana Markovic (the influential wife of Milosevic) dies in Russia.

2021 **June** Mladic appeal dismissed. Sentence confirmed.

FURTHER READING

Wesley Clark. 2002. *Waging Modern War.* New York: Public Affairs.

Zlata Filipovic. 1995. *Zlata's Diary – A Child's Life in Sarajevo.* London: Puffin Books.

Misha Glenny. 1996. *The Fall of Yugoslavia.* London: Penguin Books.

Misha Glenny. 2001. *The Balkans 1804–1999: Nationalism, War and the Great Powers.* London: Penguin Books.

James Gow. 2003. *The Serbian Project and its Adversaries: A Strategy of War Crimes.* London: Hurst and Company.

Miroslav Hadzic. 2002. *The Yugoslav People's Agony: The Role of the Yugoslav People's Army.* London: Ashgate.

Michael Ignatieff. 2001. *Virtual War.* London: Vintage.

Tim Judah. 2000. *The Serbs: History, Myth and the Destruction of Yugoslavia.* London: Yale University Press.

Jasmin Mujanovic. 2018. *Hunger and Fury: The Crisis of Democracy in the Balkans.* Oxford: Oxford University Press.

Report of the Secretary-General Pursuant to General Assembly Resolution 53/35, The Fall of Srebrenica, A/54/549 (1999).

Nick Richardson. 2002. *No Escape Zone.* London: Time Warner Paperback.

Carole Rogel. 1998. *The Breakup of Yugoslavia and the War in Bosnia.* London: The Greenwood Press.

Michael Rose. 1998. *Fighting for Peace: Lessons from Bosnia.* London: Warner Books.

Brendan Simms. 2002. *Unfinest Hour: Britain and the Destruction of Bosnia.* London: Penguin Books.

Charles Shrader. 2003. *The Muslim-Croat Civil War in Central Bosnia: A Military History, 1992–1994.* College Station: Texas A & M University Press.

Milos Stankovic. 2001. *Trusted Mole: A Soldier's Journey into Bosnia's Heart of Darkness.* London: HarperCollins.

Bob Stewart. 1993. *Broken Lives: A Personal View of the Bosnian Conflict.* London: HarperCollins.

Marcus Tanner. 2001. *Croatia: A Nation Forged in War.* London: Yale University Press.

LIST OF ABBREVIATIONS

ABiH	Armed Forces of Bosnia-Herzegovina
APC	Armoured personnel carrier
APDS	Armour piercing discarding sabot
CINCSOUTH	Commander in Chief Allied Forces South
COHA	Cessation of Hostilities Agreement
CSCE	Conference on Security and Cooperation in Europe
EC	European Community
EU	European Union
HOS	Military branch of the Croatian Party of Rights (HSP)
HV	Croatian Army
HVO	Croatian Defence Council
ICRC	International Committee of the Red Cross
ICTY	International Criminal Tribunal for the former Yugoslavia
IFOR	Implementation Force
IMF	International Monetary Fund
JDAM	Joint Direct Attack Munition
JNA	Yugoslav People's Army
MRE	Meals Ready To Eat
MPRI	Military Professional Resources Incorporated
NATO	North Atlantic Treaty Organisation
NGO	Non-Governmental Organisation
OHR	Office of the High Representative
OP	Observation Post
OSCE	Organisation for Security and Cooperation in Europe
OR RSK	Armed Forces of the Republic of Serbian Krajina
RS	Republika Srpska
RSK	Republika Srpska Krajina (Republic of Serbian Krajina)
SAS	Special Air Service
SFOR	Stabilisation Force
SACEUR	Supreme Allied Commander, Europe
TOW	Tube-launched, Optically tracked, Wire-guided

UN	United Nations
UNHCR	United Nations High Commissioner for Refugees
UNMO	United Nations Military Observer
UNPA	United Nations Protected Area
UNPROFOR	United Nations Protection Force
UNSCR	United Nations Security Council Resolution
VOPP	Vance-Owen Peace Plan
VJ	Army of Yugoslavia
VRS	Bosnian Serb Military
WEU	Western European Union

GLOSSARY OF NAMES

Fikret Abdic	Rogue Bosniak leader, Bihac pocket
Yasushi Akashi	UN special envoy
Kofi Annan	UN Secretary General
Arkan	Serbian paramilitary
Carl Bildt	EU Representative
Tony Blair	British Prime Minister
Mate Boban	Bosnian Croat leader
Boutros Boutros-Ghali	UN Secretary General
Francis Briquemont	General, Belgium Army, UNPROFOR
Momir Bulatovic	President of Montenegro
George Bush Snr	President of the United States
Lord Carrington	EC diplomat
Wesley Clark	General, US Army, SACEUR
William 'Bill' Clinton	President of the United States
Ejup Ganic	Vice-President, Bosnia-Herzegovina
Kiro Gligorov	President of Macedonia
Richard Holbrooke	Assistant Secretary of State
Douglas Hurd	British Foreign Secretary
Alija Izetbegovic	President of Bosnia-Herzegovina
Sir Michael Jackson	General, British Army, KFOR (Kosovo Force)
Bernard Janvier	General, French Army, UNPROFOR
George Joulwan	General, US Army, SACEUR
Radovan Karadzic	President of the Bosnian Serbs
Thom Karremans	Lieutenant-Colonel, Dutch Army, UNPROFOR
Milan Kucan	President of Slovenia
Lewis MacKenzie	General, Canadian Army, UNPROFOR
John Major	British Prime Minister
Ante Markovic	Prime Minister of the Yugoslav Federation
Slobodan Milosevic	President of Serbia
Ratko Mladic	General, Bosnian Serb Army
Philippe Morillon	General, French Army, UNPROFOR

Lord Owen	EC diplomat
Javier Perez de Cuellar	UN Secretary General
Sir Michael Rose	General, British Army, UNPROFOR
Vojislav Seselj	Serbian ultra-nationalist
Haris Silajdzic	Bosniac Foreign Minister
Sir Rupert Smith	General, British Army, UNPROFOR
Franjo Tudjman	President of Croatia
Cyrus Vance	UN diplomat
Boris Yeltsin	President of the Russian Federation

INDEX